Healthy Diet Guide for Elderly with Diabetes

Sidney .K Andrews

Funny helpful tips:

Stay present; the current moment is where life truly happens.

Master the art of active listening; it strengthens relationships and fosters understanding.

Healthy Diet Guide for Elderly with Diabetes : Nutrition Plans and Recipes to Manage Blood Sugar Levels in Senior Citizens with Diabetes.

Life advices:

Harness the capabilities of adaptive AI; its ability to modify its behavior offers more personalized user experiences.

Your essence shines brightest when you're true to yourself; never dim your light for the sake of fitting in.

Introduction

This is a comprehensive guide that provides individuals with diabetes, especially those new to managing their condition, a collection of recipes and meal preparation strategies to help maintain balanced blood sugar levels. Below is a brief summary of the content:

The guide offers a variety of appetizers and side dish recipes suitable for diabetics. These recipes are designed to be both delicious and supportive of blood sugar management.

Moving on to poultry recipes, the guide includes a selection of dishes featuring chicken and turkey. These recipes are mindful of diabetes-friendly ingredients and portion control.

Air-fry recipes are also incorporated into the meal prep options, providing individuals with a healthier cooking method that reduces the use of oil and promotes better eating choices.

Beef recipes are another category within the guide, offering a range of options for those who enjoy beef while managing diabetes. These recipes focus on lean cuts and smart cooking techniques.

Similar to beef, pork recipes are included with a focus on healthier preparations. The guide also introduces air fryer recipes to provide additional cooking alternatives.

For those who appreciate lamb, the guide features lamb recipes suitable for individuals with diabetes. These dishes aim to balance flavor and nutritional considerations.

The guide doesn't forget seafood lovers, offering fish and seafood recipes that are both delicious and supportive of diabetic dietary needs. Air fryer recipes for seafood are also included.

A section on vegetable-based recipes emphasizes the importance of including plenty of vegetables in a diabetic diet. These recipes are rich in nutrients and fiber.

Salad recipes provide refreshing and nutritious options for those looking to incorporate more greens into their meals. These salads are designed with diabetes management in mind.

Even individuals with diabetes can enjoy desserts in moderation. The guide includes dessert recipes that are mindful of sugar content and portion control.

To enhance the variety of cooking methods, air fryer recipes are integrated throughout the guide, promoting a healthier way of preparing meals without sacrificing flavor.

In summary, this book offers a diverse range of recipes and meal preparation ideas tailored to individuals managing diabetes. These recipes take into account nutritional considerations while providing tasty options for maintaining balanced blood sugar levels.

Contents

APPETIZERS AND SIDES 1

POULTRY RECIPES..56

AIR-FRY RECIPES 74

BEEF RECIPES...102

AIR FRY RECIPES 116

PORK RECIPES..123

AIR FRY RECIPES 134

LAMB RECIPES 142

FISH AND SEAFOOD RECIPES 156

AIR FRY RECIPES 182

VEGETABLES 209

SALADS...218

DESSERTS..223

AIR FRY RECIPES 229

APPETIZERS AND SIDES

Cucumber Rolls

Prep Time: 15 mins

Servings: 20 rolls

Ingredients:

- *1 avocado*
- *Quarter tsp salt*
- *One pinch black pepper*
- *One tsp lemon juice*
- *Half medium tomato – diced finely*
- *One Lebanese cucumber*
- *Half cup alfalfa sprouts*
- *toothpicks*

Instructions

Using a sharp knife, carefully cut the cucumber into thin horizontal slices to be used as a wrap.

In a bowl, put the avocado, salt, pepper, lemon juice, and tomato and mix well together.

Lay down one of the cucumber slices to make the rolls, place some alfalfa in the center, topped by a small spoonful of the mixture of avocado.

Roll the top of the cucumber over all the mixture and keep the edges together with a toothpick to prevent it from unrolling.

Serve on a dish or platter.

Nutrition: 77 Kcal, Protein 4 g, Carbs 5 g, Fat 6 g

Meatball Appetizers with Apricot Dip

Prep Time: 15 mins

Cook Time: 20 mins

Servings: 8

Ingredients:

- *One pound Ground Beef*
- *Quarter cup seasoned dry bread crumbs*
- *Two egg whites or one egg, beaten*
- *Two tsp water*
- *Quarter tsp salt*
- *One eighth tsp pepper*
- *Three quarter cup apricot preserves*
- *Three quarter cup barbecue sauce*
- *Two tsp Dijon-style mustard*

Instructions

Heat the stove to 400F. In a wide bowl, add the grounded beef, bread crumbs, egg whites, water, salt, and pepper, stirring gently yet thoroughly. Form them into 36 1-quarter-inch meatballs. In a broiler pan that has been coated with cooking spray, put it on a shelf. Bake in the oven at 400F for 15 to 17 minutes.

In the meanwhile, in a saucepan add barbecue sauce and mustard over low heat. Take to a boil; reduce heat; simmer 3 to 5 minutes, uncovered, stirring regularly, or until the sauce is gently thickened. Insert cooked meatballs and proceed to cook 2 to 3 minutes or, stirring regularly, until meatballs are heated through. In a slow cooker, serve or hold warm.

Place in a two-half-quart slow cooker set on LOW to hold meatballs soft. To conserve heat, keep it covered. It is possible to hold meatballs for up to 2 hours, stirring regularly.

Nutrition: 44 Kcal, Protein 2 g, Carbs 6 g, Fat 0.9 g

Antipasto Skewers

Prep Time: 15 mins

Servings: 12 skewers

Ingredients:

- *Twelve rosemary stems*
- *Twelve oz mozzarella balls*
- *Fourteen oz artichoke hearts, cut in quarters*
- *Six oz black olives, canned*
- *Twelve oz salami sliced*
- *Four oz balsamic dressing*

Instructions

Strip the rosemary stems at either end of the stem, leaving one to two-inch leaves.
Pierce cheese cubes along with the end of the rosemary stem, artichoke hearts, olives, and salami.
Drizzle with balsamic dressing skewers.
Serve instantly or refrigerate.

Nutrition: 203 Kcal, Protein 8 g, Carbs 3.8 g, Fat 15 g

Bacon and Mushroom Bite-Size Quiche

Prep Time: 45 mins
                    Cook Time: 20 mins

Servings: 1 quiche

Ingredients:

- *Eight slices bacon*
- *Quarter pound fresh mushrooms, chopped*
- *One tablespoon butter*
- *One-third cup chopped green onion*
- *Two-third cup shredded swiss cheese*
- *For double-crust pie, use homemade or purchased*
- *Five eggs*
- *Two-third cup sour cream*

Instructions
Preheat oven to 375 degrees F.
Roll out the pastry dough 1/16-inch thick on a lightly floured board.
Cut out 42 circles using a 3-inch cutter; re-roll scraps as required.
Fit circles of thinly greased two-half-inch muffin pans into the bottoms
Meanwhile, until crisp, drain, fry the bacon slices, crumble or chop.

Chop the mushrooms and sauté until limp and liquid disappears in the butter.

Combine the bacon, green onion, mushrooms, and cheese. Divide the filling uniformly between the muffin cups.

Beat the eggs together in a big cup, apply the sour cream and whisk until smooth. Into each muffin cup, add about 1 tablespoon.

Bake for 20-25 minutes until puffed and light brown. Cool for 5 minutes in pans; lift out.

Serve warm.

Nutrition: 93 Kcal, Protein 2.8 g, Carbs 3.7 g, Fat 6.1 g

Baked Beef Wonton

Prep Time: 25 mins
                Cook Time: 15 mins

Servings: 8

Ingredients:

- *Half pound lean ground beef*
- *Quarter cup finely chopped onion*
- *Quarter tsp Cajun seasoning*
- *Quarter tsp kosher salt*
- *Quarter tsp ground black pepper*
- *Quarter cup canned low-salt yellow corn, drained*
- *One-third cup salsa*
- *Twenty wonton wrappers*
- *Cooking spray*
- *Low-fat sour cream (optional)*
- *One tablespoon tomato paste*

Instructions

Preheat oven to 400F.

Cook ground beef, onion, Cajun seasoning, and salt in a large nonstick skillet 5 minutes or until beef is browned. Add corn, salsa and tomato paste and cook until heated through. Remove and allow to cool.

Working with one wonton wrapper at a time, pour 1 tablespoon beef mixture into center of each wrapper. Join 2 opposite corners and pinch tips together to seal, forming a triangle. Place wrappers on a wire rack and repeat with remaining wrappers and beef mixture. Place wonton on lightly greased baking sheets and lightly coat with cooking spray. Bake 4 to 6 minutes on each side, turning once or until golden brown. Serve with sour cream, if desired.

Nutrition: 196 Kcal, Protein 10 g, Carbs 12.1 g, Fat 10.9 g

Bruschetta

Prep Time: 10 mins

Cook Time: 10 mins

Servings: 8

Ingredients:

- one-third cup olive oil
- 4 cloves garlic, crushed
- 6 fresh basil leaves, chopped
- 1/8 tsp crushed red-pepper flakes
- Tomato Topping
- 1-Half pounds plum tomatoes, chopped
- Half cup chopped fresh basil
- 1 tablespoon balsamic vinegar
- 1 tablespoon olive oil
- Half tsp salt

- *quarter tsp black pepper*
- *one loaf French Bread (eight ounces) split horizontally*

Instructions

Start preparing seasoning oil: Heat oil over medium-low heat in a small skillet. Apply the flakes of garlic, basil, and red pepper; cook and mix for 5 to 7 minutes or until the garlic is golden brown. Then cool the oil and strain.

Meanwhile, make the tomato topping: In a big cup, add the tomatoes, basil, vinegar, oil, pepper, and salt.

Heat to 500 degrees F. the oven.

Brush cut sides of split bread with seasoning oil of about two tablespoons. Put a baking sheet over it. Bake at a heat of 500 degrees F. Bake for 3 to 5 minutes or until golden brown.

Slice two-inch widths of toasted bread and put on a wide serving platter. Top the tomatoes paste with a spoon and garnish with fresh basil leaves.

Nutrition: 16 Kcal, Protein 0 g, Carbs 1.1 g, Fat 1.1 g

Tandoori Chicken Skewers with Mint

Prep Time: 1 hour and 10 mins
   Cook Time: 15 mins

Servings: 12 skewers

Ingredients:

- *One cup fat-free plain Greek yogurt*
- *One-third cup reduced-fat coconut milk*
- *Two tsp. Curry powder, mild*

- *Three fourth tsp. Sea salt, divided*
- *One tablespoon canola oil*
- *One pound skinless and boneless chicken breast*
- *Two tablespoons finely chopped red onion*
- *Two tablespoons chopped fresh mint*
- *One tsp fresh lime juice*
- *Twelve (eight-inch) bamboo skewers*
- *One to two finely chopped garlic cloves*

Instructions

Mix two tbsp of yogurt with two tablespoons of coconut milk, curry powder, garlic, and half a tsp of salt in a big, shallow bowl or deep plate. Mix with the oil.

Cut the chicken into 12 strips lengthwise. Insert the skewer into the bottom of one strip of chicken and work it out to the maximum lengthwise. Repeat for the chicken that remains. Place skewers in the curry marinade and make sure to coat them with your fingers. Cover and refrigerate for one to eight hours with plastic wrap. Arrange on paper toweling and blot dry marinated chicken, eliminating all extra marinade. Over medium-high pressure, heat a broad skillet, and then cover with the cooking oil. Arrange the skewers in the skillet and cook the chicken until the thickest portion of the chicken is opaque and warm around the skewer. Place skewers on the serving tray.

When cooking chicken, prepare the Raita. Mix the leftover yogurt and coconut milk with the onions, mint, lime juice, and the leftover salt in a cup. To enable its flavors to develop and meld, make Raita 30 minutes before serving chicken if possible.

Nutrition: 120 Kcal, Protein 7 g, Carbs 6.5 g, Fat 6.9 g

Hummus and Tomatoes Cucumber Bites

Prep Time: 10 mins

Cook Time: 10 mins

Servings: 2

Ingredients:

- *One English cucumber*
- *Six mini tomatoes*
- *Three oz roasted red pepper hummus*
- *Fresh chopped parsley*

Instructions

Slice the cucumber into rounds and the tomatoes crosswise thinly.
On the cucumber slices, spread the hummus evenly, then cover with the tomato slices.
Use new chopped parsley to sprinkle over.

Nutrition: 147 Kcal, Protein 4 g, Carbs 15 g, Fat 7 g

Cheese Stuffed Tomato Bites

Prep Time: 5 mins

Servings: 5

Ingredients:

- *Ten cherry tomatoes, halved, with seeds and flesh removed*
- *Half cup garlic-herb cheese spread*
- *Chopped parsley for garnish*

Instructions

Put tomato halves on the platter for serving.
Put about one tablespoon cheese into each tomato half. Garnish with parsley and serve.

Nutrition: 84 Kcal, Protein 2.1 g, Carbs 2 g, Fat 7.2 g

Rice Cakes with Fire Jelly

Prep Time: 5 mins

Servings: 4

Ingredients:

- *One-third cup sugar-free apricot preserves*
- *two tablespoons minced fresh jalapeño chili pepper*
- *twelve eaches miniature salt-and-pepper rice cakes*
- *One-third cup fat-free cream cheese*
- *One tablespoon fresh rosemary, chopped*

Instructions

Mix sugar-free preserves and chili pepper in a small bowl. Then place rice cakes with cream cheese; use the preserve mixture for topping. Sprinkle with rosemary at the end.

Nutrition: 55 Kcal, Protein 3.4 g, Carbs 11.2 g, Fat 0.8 g

Cheese Casserole

Prep Time: 5 mins

Cook Time: 35 mins

Servings: 12

Ingredients:

- *Six large eggs*
- *Quarter cup milk*

- *Twelve cauliflower tots*
- *Half cup mild cheddar cheese*
- *Half cup canned mushroom*

Instructions

Spray nine-inch casserole dish with cooking oil. Use a mixer to combine all ingredients.
Pour the mixture into the casserole dish.
Bake into oven preheated at 425 degrees F for thirty to thirty-five minutes.

Nutrition: 235 Kcal, Protein 10.4 g, Carbs 10.3 g, Fat 23.8 g

Baked Carrots

Prep Time: 5 mins

Cook Time: 30 mins

Servings: 2

Ingredients:

- *Fourteen ounces carrots*
- *One tablespoon olive oil*
- *One tablespoon fresh thyme leaf*
- *Half teaspoon ground cumin*

Instructions
Oven to be preheated moderately.
Peel and cut the carrots into slices, and put them in a large bowl with the olive oil, thyme, and cumin and mix well.
Put the carrots on a baking tray and put that tray into the oven for approx. thirty minutes till it gets tender.

Nutrition: 151 Kcal, Protein 2.3 g, Carbs 0.3 g, Fat 6.4 g

Balsamic Roasted Vegetables

Prep Time: 5 mins

Cook Time: 20 mins

Servings: 2

Ingredients:

- *Two zucchinis cut lengthwise and in half*
- *Five large carrots cut lengthwise and in half*
- *Two heads of broccoli*
- *Two tablespoons balsamic vinegar*
- *Half teaspoon salt*

Instructions

Put vegetables in a baking dish. Spray with balsamic vinegar and add a pinch of salt.

Bake at 400 degrees F for twenty to twenty-five minutes till vegetables become tender.

Serve hot.

Nutrition: 38.7 Kcal, Protein 1.6 g, Carbs 8.1 g, Fat 2 g

Baked Rosemary Artichokes

Prep Time: 10 mins

Cook Time: 50 mins

Servings: 4

Ingredients:

- *Two artichokes*

- *Four tablespoons of olive oil*
- *One tablespoon minced garlic*
- *One tablespoon dried rosemary*

Instructions

Oven to be preheated to 350 degrees F.

Cut each artichoke in half on a cutting board. Take a small frying pan and slightly warm the olive oil on low/ medium heat. Add garlic and rosemary and heat for an another one to two minutes.

Cover a 9×9 glass pyrex with olive oil and spread the artichokes. Spray the flavored olive oil onto each of the halved artichoke.

Let artichokes bake in the oven for 45 minutes until they are soft.

Nutrition: 121 Kcal, Protein 0 g, Carbs 1 g, Fat 11 g

Pesto Cauliflower

Prep **Time:** **10 mins**

Cook Time: 25 mins

Servings: 4

Ingredients:

- *Four cups Cauliflower*
- *One-quarter cup pesto sauce*
- *One-quarter cup parmesan cheese*
- *Add salt and pepper to taste*

Instructions

Mix the pesto sauce and cauliflower in a mixing dish. Mix until the cauliflower is covered in pesto sauce.

Cauliflower to be spread uniformly on the baking sheet. To taste, apply salt and pepper and parmesan cheese to be used as a

topping.
Bake at 350 degrees for 25–30 minutes.

Nutrition: 99 Kcal, Protein 2.9 g, Carbs 4.8 g, Fat 8.7 g

Roast Cauliflower

Prep Time: 5 mins

Cook Time: 30 mins

Servings: 4

Ingredients:

- *One cauliflower (approx. 600 grams/twenty-one ounces)*
- *Two tablespoons olive oil*
- *One fourth tablespoon cumin*
- *One fourth tablespoon chili powder*
- *One fourth tablespoon turmeric*
- *Two cups baby spinach*

Instructions
Oven to be preheated to 370 ° F.
Cut the cauliflower into slices and be spread on a baking tray. Spray olive oil over the cauliflower.
Put the tray into the oven for twenty to thirty minutes.
Take out the tray from the oven, apply the spinach over the top, and put it back into the oven for five to ten minutes till the wilting of the spinach.

Nutrition: 106 Kcal, Protein 2.3 g, Carbs 5.9 g, Fat 7.9 g

Garlic Asparagus

Prep Time: 5 mins

Cook Time: 15 mins

Servings: 4

Ingredients:

- *sixteen asparagus*
- *Two cloves of garlic, minced*
- *Half a medium onion, diced*
- *Salt and pepper to taste*
- *Two tablespoons of olive oil*

Instructions

Preheat oven to 325 F.

Mix well the minced garlic and olive oil.

Cover a baking sheet with parchment paper, add the asparagus and cover with the olive oil and garlic mixture.

Add the diced onion, salt and pepper to taste.

Put the baking sheet in the oven and bake for fifteen to twenty minutes.

Nutrition: 47.2 Kcal, Protein 2.6 g, Carbs 5.4 g, Fat 2.3 g

Roasted Brussels Sprouts

Prep Time: 5 mins

Cook Time: 15 mins

Servings: 2

Ingredients:

- *Three bacon strips*
- *¼ cup dried cranberries*
- *Half cup of Brussel sprouts*

Instructions

Fry the bacon strips in a medium-sized pan, then remove them from the pan for later use.

Slice the Brussels sprouts in half on a cutting board and fry them for 10-15 minutes in the bacon grease left over from the fried bacon.

Crumble the cooked bacon on top and add dried cranberries once the Brussels sprouts have been cooked.

Nutrition: 134 Kcal, Protein 4 g, Carbs 10.2 g, Fat 9.7 g

Roasted Italian Green Beans & Tomatoes

Prep Time: 5 mins

Cook Time: 15 mins

Servings: 4

Ingredients:

- *Half pound fresh green beans, trimmed and halved*
- *Half pound tomatoes, trimmed*
- *One tablespoon olive oil*
- *One tablespoon Italian seasoning*

Instructions

Heat oven to 425 degrees F. Put green beans in a 15x10x1-inches baking pan. The baking pan should be coated with cooking spray. Then mix oil, Italian seasoning, and salt. Sprinkle it over beans and bake for 10 minutes.

Insert tomatoes into the pan. Beans should be roasted until they become crisp-tender, and tomatoes are softened by leaving them for an additional four to six minutes.

Nutrition: 53.1 Kcal, Protein 1.9 g, Carbs 11.8 g, Fat 0.1 g

Roasted Butternut Squash & Brussels Sprouts

Prep Time: 10 mins

Cook Time: 45 mins

Servings: 4

Ingredients:

- *Half butternut squash, cubed*
- *Two cups Brussels sprouts, sliced in half*
- *One tablespoon olive oil*
- *Salt and pepper to taste*

Instructions

Heat oven to 350 F.

Peel the skin of the butternut squash on a cutting board, then dice into cubes.

In a 9 x 11 inches glass pan, combine together butternut squash and Brussel sprouts.

Put olive oil, salt, and pepper into the pan and mix well.

Put the pan in the oven and bake for 45 minutes until the butternut squash has softened.

Nutrition: 55.1 Kcal, Protein 2.1 g, Carbs 10.3 g, Fat 0.7 g

Quinoa Muffins

Prep **time:** **10 minutes**

Cook time: 30 minutes

Servings: 12

Ingredients:

- *1 cup quinoa, cooked*

- *6 eggs, whisked*
- *Salt and pepper to the taste*

- *1 cup Swiss cheese, grated*
- *1 small yellow onion, chopped*
- *1 cup white mushrooms, sliced*
- *½ cup sun-dried tomatoes, chopped*

Instructions:

In a bowl, combine the eggs with salt, pepper and the rest of the ingredients and whisk well.

Divide this into a silicone muffin pan, bake at 350 degrees F for 30 minutes and serve for breakfast.

Nutrition: Calories 123, Fat 5.6 g, Carbs 10.8 g, Protein 7.5 g

Stuffed Tomatoes

Prep time: 10 minutes

   Cook time: 15 minutes

Servings: 4

Ingredients:

- *2 tablespoons olive oil*
- *8 tomatoes, insides scooped*
- *¼ cup almond milk*
- *8 eggs*
- *¼ cup parmesan, grated*
- *Salt and black pepper to the taste*
- *4 tablespoons rosemary, chopped*

Instructions:

Grease a pan with the oil and arrange the tomatoes inside.

Crack an egg in each tomato, divide the milk and the rest of the ingredients, introduce the pan in the oven and bake at 375 degrees F for 15 minutes.

Nutrition: Calories 276, Fat 20.3 g, Carbs 13.2 g, Protein 13.7 g

Scrambled Eggs

Prep   time: 10 minutes
        Cook time: 10 minutes
Servings: 2

Ingredients:

- *1 yellow bell pepper, chopped*
- *8 cherry tomatoes, cubed*
- *2 spring onions, chopped*
- *1 tablespoon olive oil*
- *1 tablespoon capers, drained*
- *2 tablespoons black olives, pitted and sliced*
- *4 eggs*
- *A pinch of salt and black pepper*
- *¼ teaspoon oregano, dried*
- *1 tablespoon parsley, chopped*

Instructions:
Heat up a pan with the oil over medium-high heat, add the bell pepper and spring onions and sauté for 3 minutes.
Add the tomatoes, capers and the olives and sauté for 2 minutes more.
Crack the eggs into the pan, add salt, pepper and the oregano and scramble for 5 minutes more.
Divide the scramble between plates, sprinkle the parsley on top and serve.

Nutrition: Calories 249, Fat 17 g, Carbs 13.3 g, Protein 13.5 g

Ham Muffins

Prep time: 10 minutes

Cook time: 15 minutes

Servings: 6

Ingredients:

- *9 ham slices*
- *5 eggs, whisked*
- *1/3 cup spinach, chopped*
- *¼ cup feta cheese, crumbled*
- *½ cup roasted red peppers, chopped*
- *A pinch of salt and black pepper*
- *1 and ½ tablespoons basil pesto*
- *Cooking spray*

Instructions:

Grease a muffin tin with cooking spray and line each muffin mould with 1 and ½ ham slices.

Divide the peppers and the rest of the ingredients except the eggs, pesto, salt and pepper into the ham cups.

In a bowl, mix the eggs with the pesto, salt and pepper, whisk and pour over the peppers mix.

Bake the muffins in the oven at 400 degrees F for 15 minutes and serve for breakfast.

Nutrition: Calories 109, Fat 6.7 g, Carbs 1.8 g, Protein 9.3 g

Avocado Spread

Prep   **time:**   **5 minutes**

Servings: 8

Ingredients:

- 2 avocados, peeled, pitted and roughly chopped
- 1 tablespoon sun-dried tomatoes, chopped
- 2 tablespoons lemon juice
- 3 tablespoons cherry tomatoes, chopped
- ¼ cup red onion, chopped
- 1 teaspoon oregano, dried
- 2 tablespoons parsley, chopped
- 4 kalamata olives, pitted and chopped
- A pinch of salt and black pepper

Instructions:

Put the avocados in a bowl and mash with a fork.

Add the rest of the ingredients, stir to combine and serve as a morning spread.

Nutrition: Calories 110, Fat 10 g, Carbs 5.7 g, Protein 1.2 g

Baked Omelet Mix

Prep time: 10 minutes   **Cook time: 45 minutes Servings: 12**

Ingredients:

- 12 eggs, whisked
- 8 ounces spinach, chopped
- 2 cups almond milk
- 12 ounces canned artichokes, chopped
- 2 garlic cloves, minced
- 5 ounces feta cheese, crumbled
- 1 tablespoon dill, chopped
- 1 teaspoon oregano, dried

- 1 teaspoon lemon pepper
- A pinch of salt
- 4 teaspoons olive oil

Instructions:

Heat up a pan with the oil over medium-high heat, add the garlic and the spinach and sauté for 3 minutes.

In a baking dish, combine the eggs with the artichokes and the rest of the ingredients.

Add the spinach mix as well, toss a bit, bake the mix at 375 degrees F for 40 minutes, divide between plates and serve for breakfast.

Nutrition: Calories 186, Fat 13 g, Carbs 5 g, Protein 10 g

Tuna Salad

Prep time: 10 minutes   **Servings: 2**

Ingredients:

- 12 ounces canned tuna in water, drained and flaked
- ¼ cup roasted red peppers, chopped
- 2 tablespoons capers, drained
- 8 kalamata olives, pitted and sliced
- 2 tablespoons olive oil
- 1 tablespoon parsley, chopped
- 1 tablespoon lemon juice
- A pinch of salt and black pepper

Instructions:

In a bowl, combine the tuna with roasted peppers and the rest of the ingredients, toss, divide between plates and serve for breakfast.

Nutrition: Calories 250, Fat 17.3 g, Carbs 2.7 g, Protein 10.1 g

Veggie Quiche

Prep time: 6 minutes   **Cook time: 55**
minutes Servings: 8

Ingredients:

- *½ cup sun-dried tomatoes, chopped*
- *1 prepared pie crust*
- *2 tablespoons avocado oil*
- *1 yellow onion, chopped*
- *2 garlic cloves, minced*
- *2 cups spinach, chopped*
- *1 red bell pepper, chopped*
- *¼ cup kalamata olives, pitted and sliced*
- *1 teaspoon parsley flakes*
- *1 teaspoon oregano, dried*
- *1/3 cup feta cheese, crumbled*
- *4 eggs, whisked*
- *1 and ½ cups almond milk*
- *1 cup cheddar cheese, shredded*
- *Salt and black pepper to the taste*

Instructions:

Heat up a pan with the oil over medium-high heat, add the garlic and onion and sauté for 3 minutes.

Add the bell pepper and sauté for 3 minutes more.

Add the olives, parsley, spinach, oregano, salt and pepper and cook everything for 5 minutes.

Add tomatoes and the cheese, toss and take off the heat.

Arrange the pie crust in a pie plate, pour the spinach and tomatoes mix inside and spread.

In a bowl, mix the eggs with salt, pepper, the milk and half of the cheese, whisk and pour over the mixture in the pie crust.

Sprinkle the remaining cheese on top and bake at 375 degrees F for 40 minutes.

Cool the quiche down, slice and serve for breakfast.

Nutrition: Calories 211, Fat 14.4 g, Carbs 12.5 g, Protein 8.6 g

Leeks and Eggs Muffins

Prep time: 10 minutes   **Cook time: 20 minutes**
Servings: 2

Ingredients:

- 3 eggs, whisked
- ¼ cup baby spinach
- 2 tablespoons leeks, chopped
- 4 tablespoons parmesan, grated
- 2 tablespoons almond milk
- Cooking spray
- 1 small red bell pepper, chopped
- Salt and black pepper to the taste
- 1 tomato, cubed
- 2 tablespoons cheddar cheese, grated

Instructions:
In a bowl, combine the eggs with the milk, salt, pepper and the rest of the ingredients except the cooking spray and whisk well.
Grease a muffin tin with the cooking spray and divide the eggs mixture in each muffin mould.
Bake at 380 degrees F for 20 minutes and serve them for breakfast.

Nutrition: Calories 308, Fat 19.4 g, Carbs 8.7 g, Protein 24.4 g

Eggplant Salad

Prep Time: 20 minutes   **Cook Time: 15**
minutes Servings: 8

Ingredients:

- *1 large eggplant, washed and cubed*
- *1 tomato, seeded and chopped*
- *1 small onion, diced*

- *2 tablespoons parsley, chopped*
- *2 tablespoons extra virgin olive oil*
- *2 tablespoons distilled white vinegar*
- *½ cup feta cheese, crumbled*
- *Salt as needed*

Instructions:
Preheat your outdoor grill to medium-high.
Pierce the eggplant a few times using a knife/fork.
Cook the eggplants on your grill for about 15 minutes until they are charred.
Keep it on the side and allow them to cool.
Remove the skin from the eggplant and dice the pulp.
Transfer the pulp to a mixing bowl and add parsley, onion, tomato, olive oil, feta cheese and vinegar.
Mix well and chill for 1 hour.
Season with salt and enjoy!

Nutrition: Calories: 99 Fat: 7 g Carbs: 7 g Protein: 3.4 g

Artichoke Frittata

Prep Time: 5 minutes   **Cook Time: 10**
minutes Servings: 4

Ingredients:

- *8 large eggs*
- *¼ cup Asiago cheese, grated*
- *1 tablespoon fresh basil, chopped*
- *1 teaspoon fresh oregano, chopped*

- *Pinch of salt*
- *1 teaspoon extra virgin olive oil*
- *1 teaspoon garlic, minced*
- *1 cup canned artichoke*
- *es, drained*
- *1 tomato, chopped*

Instructions:
Pre-heat your oven to broil.
Take a medium bowl and whisk in eggs, Asiago cheese, oregano, basil, sea salt and pepper.
Blend in a bowl.
Place a large ovenproof skillet over medium-high heat and add olive oil.
Add garlic and sauté for 1 minute.
Remove skillet from heat and pour in egg mix.
Return skillet to heat and sprinkle artichoke hearts and tomato over eggs.
Cook frittata without stirring for 8 minutes.
Place skillet under the broiler for 1 minute until the top is lightly browned.
Cut frittata into 4 pieces and serve.

Nutrition: Calories: 199 Fat: 13 g Carbs: 5 g Protein: 16 g

Cool Tomato and Dill Frittata

Prep Time: 5 minutes   **Cook Time:**
10 minutes Servings: 4

Ingredients:

- *2 tablespoons olive oil*
- *1 medium onion, chopped*
- *1 teaspoon garlic, minced*
- *2 medium tomatoes, chopped*

- 6 large eggs
- ½ cup half and half
- ½ cup feta cheese, crumbled
- ¼ cup dill weed
- Salt as needed
- Ground black pepper as needed

Instructions:

Preheat your oven to a temperature of 400 ° Fahrenheit.

Take a large-sized ovenproof pan and heat up your olive oil over medium-high heat.

Toss in the onion, garlic, tomatoes, and stir fry them for 4 minutes.

While they are being cooked, take a bowl and beat together your eggs, half and half cream and season the mix with some pepper and salt.

Pour the mixture into the pan with your vegetables and top it with crumbled feta cheese and dill weed.

Cover it with the lid and let it cook for 3 minutes.

Place the pan inside your oven and let it bake for 10 minutes.

Nutrition: Calories: 191 Fat: 15 g Carbs: 6 g Protein: 9 g

Chili Oregano Baked Cheese

Prep Time: 5 minutes   **Cook Time: 35 minutes**
Servings: 4

Ingredients:

- 8 oz. feta cheese
- 4 oz. mozzarella, crumbled
- chili pepper, sliced
- 1 tsp. dried oregano
- tbsps. olive oil

Instructions:
Place the feta cheese in a small deep-dish baking pan.

Top with the mozzarella then season with pepper slices and oregano.

Cover the pan with aluminum foil and cook in the preheated oven at 350F for 20 minutes.

Serve the cheese right away.

Nutrition: Calories 292, Fat: 24.2 g, Carbs: 3.7 g, Protein: 16.2 g

AIR-FRY RECIPES

Air Fryer Buffalo Cauliflower

Prep Time: 5 mins

Cook Time: 15 mins

Servings: 4

Ingredients:

- *½ cup homemade buffalo sauce*
- *One head of cauliflower, cut bite-size pieces*
- *Butter melted: 1 tablespoon*
- *Olive oil*
- *Kosher salt & pepper, to taste*

Instructions

Spray cooking oil on the air fryer basket.

In a bowl, add buffalo sauce, melted butter, pepper, and salt. Mix well.

Put the cauliflower bits in the air fryer and spray the olive oil over it. Let it cook at 400 ° F for 7 minutes.

Remove the cauliflower from the air fryer and add it to the sauce. Coat it well.

Put the sauce coated cauliflower back into the air fryer.

Cook at 400 ° F, for 7-8 minutes or until crispy.

Nutrition: 100 Kcal, Protein 3.3 g, Carbs 4.2 g, Fat 6.7 g

Air Fryer Mini Pizza

Prep Time: 2 mins

Cook Time: 5 mins

Servings: 1

Ingredients:

- *1/4 cup sliced olives*
- *One pita bread*
- *One tomato*
- *1/2 cup shredded cheese*

Instructions

Let the air fryer preheat to 350 °F.
Lay pita flat on a plate. Add cheese, slices of tomatoes, and olives.
Cook for five minutes at 350 °F.

Nutrition: 341 Kcal, Protein 17 g, Carbs 34 g, Fat 12 g

Air Fryer Egg Rolls

Prep Time: 10 mins

Cook Time: 20 mins

Servings: 3

Ingredients:

- *half bag coleslaw mix*
- *Half onion*
- *1/2 teaspoon salt*
- *Half cups of mushrooms*
- *2 cups lean ground pork*
- *One stalk of celery*
- *Wrappers (egg roll)*

Instructions

Put a skillet over medium flame, add onion and lean ground pork and cook for 5-7 minutes. Add coleslaw mixture, salt, mushrooms, and celery and cook for almost five minutes.

Lay egg roll and add filling (1/3 cup), roll it up, seal with water. Spray with oil.

Put in the air fryer for 6-8 minutes at 400°F, flipping once halfway through.

Serve hot.

Nutrition: 244 Kcal, Protein 10 g, Carbs 9 g, Fat 9 g

Air Fryer Chicken Nuggets

Prep Time: 15 mins

Cook Time: 15 mins

Servings: 4

Ingredients:

- *Olive oil spray*
- *2 chicken breasts, cut into bite pieces, skinless and boneless*
- *Half tsp. of kosher salt*
- *Ground black pepper, to taste*
- *2 tablespoons Grated parmesan cheese*
- *6 tablespoons of panko*
- *2 tablespoons whole wheat breadcrumbs*
- *2 teaspoons olive oil*

Instructions

Let the air fryer preheat for 8 minutes, to 400 °F

In a mixing bowl, add panko, parmesan cheese, and breadcrumbs and mix well.

Sprinkle on the chicken, salt and pepper, and olive oil. Mix well. Take a few pieces of chicken, dunk them into breadcrumbs mixture. Put these pieces in an air fryer and spray with olive oil. Cook for 8 minutes, turning halfway through.

Nutrition: 187 Kcal, Protein 24 g, Carbs 7 g, Fat 4.3 g

Chicken Tenders

Prep Time: 10 mins

Cook Time: 20 mins

Servings: 3

Ingredients:

- *4 cups chicken tenderloins*
- *1 egg*
- *½ cup Superfine Almond Flour*
- *½ cup Powdered Parmesan cheese*
- *½ teaspoon Kosher Sea salt*
- *1-teaspoon black pepper*
- *1/2 teaspoon Cajun seasoning*

Instructions
Beat the egg in a plate.
Mix almond flour, freshly ground black pepper & kosher salt and the other seasonings.
Spray the air fryer with oil spray.
Dip each tender in egg and then in flour mixture.
Place each tender in your air fryer basket and spray oil on them.
Cook for 12 minutes at 350°F, then raise temperature to 400°F to shade the surface for 3 minutes.

Nutrition: 270 Kcal, Protein 21 g, Carbs 5.5 g, Fat 9 g

Kale & Celery Crackers

Prep Time: 10 mins

Cook Time: 20 mins

Servings: 6

Ingredients:

- One cups flax seed, ground
- 1 cups flax seed, soaked overnight and drained

- 2 bunches kale, chopped
- 1 bunch basil, chopped
- ½ bunch celery, chopped
- 2 garlic cloves, minced
- 1/3 cup olive oil

Instructions

Mix the ground flaxseed with the celery, kale, basil, and garlic in your food processor and mix well.

Add the oil and soaked flaxseed, then mix again, scatter in the pan of your air fryer, break into medium crackers and cook for 20 minutes at 380 degrees F.

Nutrition: 142 Kcal, Protein 4 g, Carbs 7.8 g, Fat 9 g

Air Fryer Spanakopita Bites

Prep Time: 10 mins

Cook Time: 15 mins

Servings: 4

Ingredients:

- 4 sheets phyllo dough

- 2 cups Baby spinach leaves
- 2 tablespoons Grated Parmesan cheese
- 1/4 cup Low-fat cottage cheese
- 1 teaspoon Dried oregano
- Feta cheese: 6 tbsp. crumbled
- Water: 2 tablespoons
- One egg white only
- Lemon zest: 1 teaspoon
- Cayenne pepper: 1/8 teaspoon
- Olive oil: 1 tablespoon
- Kosher salt and black pepper: 1/4 teaspoon, each

Instructions

In a pot over high heat, add water and spinach, cook until wilted. Drain it and cool for ten minutes. Squeeze out excess water.

In a bowl, mix cottage cheese, Parmesan cheese, oregano, salt, cayenne pepper, egg white, black pepper, feta cheese, spinach, and lemon zest.

Lay one phyllo sheet on a flat surface. Spray with oil. Form 16 strips from all oiled sheets. Add one tbsp of filling on each strip. Roll it.

Spray the air fryer basket with oil. Put bites in the basket, spray with oil, and cook for 12 minutes at 375°F until crispy and golden brown. Flip halfway through.

Nutrition: 81 Kcal, Protein 4 g, Carbs 6 g, Fat 3.9 g

Air Fryer Onion Rings

Prep Time: 10 mins

Cook Time: 10 mins

Servings: 4

Ingredients:

- 1 egg whisked

- *One onion*
- *Whole-wheat breadcrumbs: 1 and 1/2 cup*

- *Smoked paprika: 1 teaspoon*
- *Flour: 1 cup*
- *Garlic powder: 1 teaspoon*
- *Buttermilk: 1 cup*
- *Kosher salt and pepper to taste*

Instructions

Cut the onion half-inch-thick rounds.

In a bowl, add flour, pepper, garlic powder, smoked paprika, and salt. Then add egg and buttermilk. Mix to combine.

In another bowl, add the breadcrumbs.

Coat the onions in buttermilk mix, then in breadcrumbs mix.

Freeze these breaded onions for 15 minutes. Spray the fryer basket with oil spray.

Put onions in the air fryer basket in one single layer. Spray the onion with cooking oil.

Cook at 370 degrees for 10-12 minutes.

Nutrition: 200 Kcal, Protein 17 g, Carbs 7 g, Fat 5.2 g

Air Fryer Squash

Prep Time: 5 mins

Cook Time: 10 mins

Servings: 4

Ingredients:

- *Olive oil: 1/2 Tablespoon*
- *One squash*
- *Salt: 1/2 teaspoon*
- *Rosemary: 1/2 teaspoon*

Instructions

Chop the squash in slices of 1/4 thickness. Discard the seeds.
In a bowl, add olive oil, salt, rosemary with squash slices. Mix well.
Cook the squash for ten minutes at 400 ° F. Flip the squash halfway through. Make sure it is cooked completely.

Nutrition: 68 Kcal, Protein 0.9 g, Carbs 8 g, Fat 4 g

Zucchini Parmesan Chips

Prep Time: 10 mins

Cook Time: 20 mins

Servings: 6

Ingredients:

- *Seasoned, whole wheat Breadcrumbs: ½ cup*
- *Two zucchinis*
- *Parmesan Cheese: ½ cup (grated)*
- *1 Egg whisked*
- *Kosher salt and pepper, to taste*

Instructions

Slice the zucchini and pat dry so that no moisture remains.
In a bowl, whisk the egg with a few tsp. of water, salt, and pepper. In another bowl, mix the grated cheese and breadcrumbs.
Coat zucchini slices in egg mix then in breadcrumbs. Put all in a rack and spray with olive oil.
In a single layer, add the zucchini in the air fryer, and cook for 8 minutes at 350 °F.

Nutrition: 100 Kcal, Protein 9 g, Carbs 6.1 g, Fat 7.5 g

Air Fryer Roasted Corn

**Prep Time: 10
mins**

Cook Time: 10 mins

Servings: 4

Ingredients:

- *4 corn ears*
- *Olive oil: 2 to 3 teaspoons*
- *Kosher salt and pepper to taste*

Instructions

Clean the corn, wash, and pat dry. Cut it if need to.
Fit it in the basket of air fryer, top with olive oil, kosher salt, and pepper, and cook for ten minutes at 400 ° F.

Nutrition: 27 Kcal, Protein 7.2 g, Carbs 0 g, Fat 1 g

Air-Fried Spinach Frittata

**Prep Time: 5
mins**

Cook Time: 10 mins

Servings: 4

Ingredients:

- *1/3 cup of spinach*
- *One chopped red onion*
- *1 shredded mozzarella cheese*
- *Three eggs*
- *Salt and pepper*

Instructions

Let the air fryer preheat to 360°F.

In a skillet over a medium flame, add oil and onion, and cook until the onion is translucent. Add spinach and sauté until half cooked. Beat eggs and season with salt and pepper and mix spinach mixture in it.

Cook in the air fryer for 8 minutes.

Nutrition: 127 Kcal, Protein 16 g, Carbs 13.2 g, Fat 10 g

Air Fried Sweet Potatoes

Prep Time: 5 mins

Cook Time: 5 mins

Servings: 2

Ingredients:

- *One sweet potato*
- *A pinch of salt and black pepper*
- *1 tsp olive oil*

Instructions

Cut the peeled potato in French fries. Coat with salt, pepper, and oil.

Cook in the air fryer for 8 minutes, at 400 degrees F.

Cook potatoes in batches, in single layers and shake the basket once or twice.

Nutrition: 61 Kcal, Protein 1 g, Carbs 11 g, Fat 5 g

Air Fried Kale Chips

Prep Time: 5 mins

Cook Time: 5 mins

Servings: 2

Ingredients:

- One bunch of kale
- Half tsp. of garlic powder
- One tsp. of olive oil
- Half tsp. of salt

Instructions

Let the air fryer preheat to 370 degrees F.

Cut the kale into small pieces and add it in a bowl, with all other ingredients.

Put kale to the air fryer and cook for three minutes. Toss it and cook for two minutes more.

Nutrition: 36 Kcal, Protein 2.8 g, Carbs 5.8 g, Fat 0.9 g

Crispy Air Fried Brussels Sprouts

Prep Time: 5 mins

Cook Time: 10 mins

Servings: 4

Ingredients:

- Almonds: 1/4 cup, sliced
- Brussel sprouts: 2 cups
- Kosher salt
- Parmesan cheese: 1/4 cup, grated
- Olive oil: 2 Tablespoons
- Bagel seasoning: 2 Tablespoons

Instructions

In a saucepan, add Brussel sprouts with two cups of water and let it cook over medium flame for almost ten minutes. Drain them and cut in half.

In a mixing bowl, add Brussel sprout with almonds, oil, salt, parmesan cheese, and bagel seasoning.
Cook in the air fryer for 12-15 minutes at 375° F.

Nutrition: 154 Kcal, Protein 6.2 g, Carbs 2.7 g, Fat 2.8 g

Vegetable Rolls

Prep Time: 10 mins
                                Cook Time: 15 mins
Servings: 4

Ingredients:

- *Toasted sesame seeds*
- *2 carrots, grated*
- *Spring roll wrappers*
- *One egg white*
- *A dash gluten-free soy sauce*
- *Half cabbage, sliced*
- *Olive oil: 2 tbsp.*

Instructions
In a pan over high flame heat, 2 tbsp. of oil and sauté the chopped vegetables. Add soy sauce, turn off the heat, and add toasted sesame seeds.
Lay rolls on a surface and spread egg white with a brush.
Add some vegetable mix in the wrapper and fold.
Spray the rolls with oil spray and cook in the Air Fryer for 8 minutes at 380°F.

Nutrition: 126 Kcal, Protein 12 g, Carbs 8.2 g, Fat 15 g

Zucchini Gratin

Prep Time: 10 mins

Cook Time: 15 mins

Servings: 4

Ingredients:

- *Olive oil: 1 tablespoon*
- *Fresh parsley, chopped: 1 tablespoon*
- *Whole wheat bread crumbs: 2 tablespoons*
- *2 zucchini*
- *Black pepper & kosher salt to taste*
- *Grated Parmesan cheese: 4 tablespoons*

Instructions

Let the air fryer preheat to 360°F.

Cut zucchini in half, and a further cut in eight pieces.

In a bowl, add cheese, pepper, parsley, bread crumbs, and oil. Mix well.

Add the mixture on top of the zucchini. Then cook in the Air Fryer for 15 minutes or until light golden brown.

Nutrition: 81 Kcal, Protein 3.5 g, Carbs 6 g, Fat 5 g

Asparagus Frittata

Prep Time: 10 mins

Cook Time: 5 mins

Servings: 2

Ingredients:

- *4 eggs, whisked*
- *3 Tablespoons Parmesan cheese, grated*
- *2 Tablespoons coconut milk*
- *Salt and black pepper to taste*

- *Ten asparagus tips, steamed*
- *Cooking spray*

Instructions
Mix well the eggs with the parmesan, butter, salt, pepper.
Heat your air fryer to 400 degrees F and spray with cooking spray.
Add asparagus, the eggs mixture. Toss a little, and cook for 5 minutes.

Nutrition: 310 Kcal, Protein 2 g, Carbs 13 g, Fat 5 g

Air Fried Bacon-Wrapped Jalapeno Poppers

Prep Time: 10 mins

Cook Time: 8 mins

Servings: 10

Ingredients:

- *Cream cheese: 1/3 cup*
- *Ten jalapenos*
- *Bacon: 5 strips*

Instructions
Let the air fryer preheat to 370 °F.
Wash and pat dry the jalapenos. Cut them in half and take out the seeds. Spread the cream cheese. Cut the bacon strips in half. Wrap the cream cheese filled jalapenos with slices of bacon. Secure with a toothpick.
Place the jalapenos in the air fryer, cook at 370 °F for 6-8 minutes.

Nutrition: 75 Kcal, Protein 3 g, Carbs 0.9 g, Fat 6.8 g

Air Fried Zucchini Chips

Prep Time: 10 mins

Cook Time: 12 mins

Servings: 2

Ingredients:

- *Parmesan Cheese: 3 Tbsp.*
- *Garlic Powder: 1/4 tsp*
- *Thin sliced zucchini: 1 Cup*
- *Corn Starch: 1/4 Cup*
- *Onion Powder: 1/4 tsp*
- *Salt: 1/4 tsp*
- *Whole wheat Bread Crumbs: 1/2 Cup*
- *Olive oil*

Instructions

Let the Air Fryer preheat to 390 ° F.

In a food processor, blend into finer pieces garlic powder, salt, bread crumbs, parmesan cheese, and onion powder.

In 2 separate bowls, add corn starch in one, and whole wheat breadcrumb in the other. Coat zucchini chips into corn starch, then coat in bread crumbs.

Spray the air fryer basket with olive oil. Add breaded zucchini chips in a single layer in the air fryer and spray with olive oil.

Air fry for six minutes at preheated temperature. Cook for another four minutes after turning zucchini chips.

Nutrition: 218 Kcal, Protein 12 g, Carbs 11 g, Fat 21 g

Air Fryer Avocado Fries

Prep Time: 10 mins

Cook Time: 10 mins

Servings: 2

Ingredients:

- *One avocado*
- *One egg*
- *Whole wheat bread crumbs: 1/2 cup*
- *Salt: 1/2 teaspoon*

Instructions

Cut avocado into wedges.

In a bowl, beat egg with salt. In another bowl, add the bread crumbs.
Coat avocado wedges in egg, then in crumbs.

Air fry at 400 °F for 8-10 minutes. Toss halfway through.

Nutrition: 249 Kcal, Protein 5 g, Carbs 18 g, Fat 16 g

Avocado Egg Rolls

Prep Time: 15 mins

Cook Time: 15 mins

Servings: 2

Ingredients:

- *Ten egg roll wrappers*
- *Diced sundried tomatoes: ¼ cup (oil drained)*
- *Avocados, cut in cube*
- *Red onion, chopped: 2/3 cup*
- *1/3 cup chopped cilantro*
- *Kosher salt and black pepper*
- *Juice of two limes*

Instructions

In a bowl, add sundried tomatoes, avocado, cilantro, lime juice, pepper, onion, and salt and mix well.

Lay egg roll wrappers flat on a surface, add ¼ cup of filling in each wrapper's bottom. Seal with water and make it into a roll and spray the rolls with olive oil.

Cook at 400 ° F in the air fryer for six minutes. Turn halfway through.

Nutrition: 159 Kcal, Protein 19 g, Carbs 5.4 g, Fat 18 g

Cheesy Bell Pepper Eggs

Prep Time: 10 mins

Cook Time: 15 mins

Servings: 4

Ingredients:

- *4 green bell peppers*
- *3 ounces cooked ham, chopped*
- *1/4 onion, peeled and chopped*
- *8 eggs*
- *1 cup mild Cheddar cheese*

Instructions

Cut each bell pepper from its tops. Pick the seeds with a small knife and the white membranes. Place onion and ham into each pepper. Break two eggs into each chili pepper. Cover with 1/4 cup of cheese. Put the basket into the air fryer. Set the temperature to 390 ° F and timer for 15 minutes.

Nutrition: 317 Kcal, Protein 24 g, Carbs 4.5 g, Fat 18.5 g

Crisp Egg Cups

Prep Time: 10 mins

Cook Time: 10 mins

Servings: 4

Ingredients:

- *Toasted whole-wheat bread: 4 slices*
- *Cooking spray*
- *4 eggs*
- *1 and a half tbsp. butter (trans-fat free)*
- *Ham: 1 thick slice*
- *Salt: 1/8 tsp*
- *Black pepper: 1/8 tsp*

Instructions

Let the air fryer Preheat to 375 ° F. Take four ramekins, and spray with cooking spray.

Trim off the crusts from bread, and add butter to one side. Put the bread down into a ramekin, with butter-side in.

Cut the ham in strips, half-inch thick, and add on top of the bread.

Add one egg to each ramekin. Add salt and pepper.

Put the custard cups in the air fryer at 375 °F for 10–13 minutes.

Nutrition: 149 Kcal, Protein 12 g, Carbs 5 g, Fat 8.1 g

Lemon-Garlic Tofu with Quinoa

Prep Time: 20 mins

Cook Time: 10 mins

Servings: 2

Ingredients:

- *Cooked quinoa: 2 cups*

- *Lemons: two zest and juice*
- *Sea salt & white pepper to taste*
- *Tofu: one block - pressed and sliced into half pieces*
- *Garlic – minced: 2 cloves*

Instructions

Add the tofu into a deep dish.

In another bowl, add the garlic, lemon juice, lemon zest, salt, pepper.

Pour this marinade over tofu. Let it marinate for at least 15 minutes.

Add the tofu to the air fryer basket.

Let it air fry at 370°F for 15 minutes. Shake the basket after 8 minutes of cooking.

In a big deep bowl, add the cooked quinoa with the lemon-garlic Tofu, and serve.

Nutrition: 186 Kcal, Protein 21 g, Carbs 7.8 g, Fat 8.5 g

Vegan Mashed Potato

Prep Time: 10 mins

Cook Time: 20 mins

Servings: 4

Ingredients:

For mashed potatoes:

- *Olive oil*
- *Red potatoes cooked with the skin on, cut into one-inch pieces*
- *1/4 tsp of salt*
- *Sea salt and black pepper - to taste*
- *Half cup of unsweetened soy milk or vegan milk*

For the Tofu:

- *One teaspoon of garlic powder*
- *One block of extra firm tofu: pressed, cut into one-inch pieces*
- *Light soy sauce:2 tablespoons*

Instructions

To make the Mashed Potatoes

Add the cooked potatoes to a large bowl, mash with masher with olive oil. Then add milk and mix well.

Cover the bowl with plastic wrap, so it will keep warm and let it rest. Meanwhile, add the tofu in one even layer in the air fryer, add the garlic and soy sauce, and make sure to cover all the tofu. Let it cook for ten minutes at 400°F.

In the bowls, add the mashed potatoes, and cover with tofu.

Nutrition: 251 Kcal, Protein 20 g, Carbs 11 g, Fat 15 g

Vegan Breakfast Sandwich

Prep Time: 10 mins

Cook Time: 10 mins

Servings: 4

Ingredients:

For Tofu:

- *Garlic powder: 1 teaspoon*
- *Light soy sauce: 1/4 cup*
- *Turmeric: 1/2 teaspoon*
- *1 block extra firm pressed tofu: cut into 4 round slices*

For sandwich:

- *4 English vegan muffins*
- *Avocado: one cut into slices*
- *4 tomato slices*

- *Vegan cheese: 4 slices*
- *1 sliced onion*
- *Vegan mayonnaise*

Instructions

In a deep dish, add the tofu circles with turmeric, soy sauce, and garlic powder. Let it for 10 minutes.

Put the marinated tofu in an air fryer. Cook for ten minutes at 400 ° F and shake the basket after 5 minutes.

Add vegan mayonnaise to the English muffins. Add vegan cheese, avocado slices, tomato, onion, and marinated, cooked tofu. Top with the other half of the English muffins.

Nutrition: 197 Kcal, Protein 19 g, Carbs 12 g, Fat 9 g

Crispy Fat-Free Potatoes

Prep Time: 10 mins

Cook Time: 35 mins

Servings: 3

Ingredients:

- *Red potatoes: 1 and 1/2 pounds*
- *Aquafaba: 1 tablespoon*
- *Tomato paste: 1 teaspoon*
- *Sea salt: 1 teaspoon*
- *Brown rice flour: half tablespoon*

- *Garlic powder: half teaspoon*
- *Sweet smoked paprika: 3/4 tsp.*

Instructions

Cut the potatoes into small quarters, making sure they are the same sized. The maximum thickness of potatoes should be one and a half-inch thick.

Boil the potatoes, drain and add them in a large bowl.

In another bowl, add tomato paste and aquafaba.

In a third bowl, mix the remaining ingredients with flour.

Now add the last two bowls to the potatoes, and coat every piece.

Preheat the air fryer to 360°F for 3 minutes, then place the potatoes in the basket and cook for 12 minutes.

Shake the basket every six minutes, making sure no potatoes get stuck on the bottom.

Nutrition: 171 Kcal, Protein 5 g, Carbs 22 g, Fat 5 g

Cheese and Veggie Air Fryer Eggs

Prep Time: 10 mins

Cook Time: 20 mins

Servings: 4

Ingredients:

- *Shredded cheese: 1 cup*
- *Non-stick cooking spray*
- *Vegetables of your choice: 1 cup diced*
- *Chopped cilantro: 1 Tbsp.*
- *Four eggs*
- *Salt and Pepper to taste*

Instructions

Take four ramekins, grease them with oil.

In a bowl, crack the eggs with half the cheese, cilantro, salt, diced vegetables, and pepper. Pour in the ramekins.

Put in the air-fryer basket and cook for 12 minutes, at 300 ° F. Then add the cheese to the cups.

Set the air-fryer at 400 degrees F and continue to cook for two minutes, until cheese is lightly browned and melted.

Nutrition: 194 Kcal, Protein 15 g, Carbs 6.5 g, Fat 11 g

Low Carb Baked Eggs

Prep Time: 10 mins

Cook Time: 15 mins

Servings: 4

Ingredients:

- *Cooking Spray*
- *Grated cheese: 1-2 teaspoons*
- *One egg*
- *Fresh sautéed spinach: 1 tablespoon*
- *Salt to taste*
- *Soy milk: 1 tablespoon*
- *Black pepper to taste*

Instructions
Take ramekins and spray them with cooking spray. Add milk, spinach, egg, and cheese.
Add salt and pepper. Stir everything but do not break the yolk.
Let it air fry for 6-12 minutes at 330 ° F.
If you want runny yolks, cook for less time.

Nutrition: 114 Kcal, Protein 11 g, Carbs 1 g, Fat 6 g

Easy Air Fryer Omelet

Prep Time: 10 mins

Cook Time: 15 mins

Servings: 2

Ingredients:

- *Breakfast Seasoning: 1 teaspoon*
- *Two eggs*
- *A pinch of salt*
- *Milk: 1/4 cup*
- *Shredded cheese: 1/4 cup*
- *Diced veggies: green onions, red bell pepper, and mushrooms*

Instructions

In a bowl, mix the milk and eggs, combine them well. Season with a pinch of salt. Add the chopped vegetables.

Add the egg mixture to a 6"x3" baking pan. Make sure it is well greased.

Put the pan in the air fryer basket. Air fry for 8-10 minutes at 350º F. After 5 minutes, add the breakfast seasoning and top with shredded cheese.

Take out from the air fryer, and transfer to the plate.

Nutrition: 226 Kcal, Protein 14 g, Carbs 7.7 g, Fat 12 g

Appetizer Bombs

Prep Time: 10 mins

Cook Time: 15 mins

Servings: 3

Ingredients:

- *Three eggs, lightly whisked*
- *Low-fat cream cheese: two tbsp. Softened*
- *Chopped chives: 1 tablespoon*
- *Freshly prepared whole-wheat pizza dough: 4 ounces*
- *Cooking spray*

- *3 pieces of bacon*

Instructions

In a skillet, cook the bacon slices for about ten minutes. Crumble them. Add the eggs to the skillet and cook for almost one minute. In a bowl, mix chives, cheese, and bacon.

Cut the dough into four pieces. Make it into a five-inch circle. Add 1/4 of egg mixture in the center of each dough circle pieces. Seal the dough seams with water and pinch.

Add dough pockets in one single layer in the air fryer. Spray with cooking oil.

Cook for 5-6 minutes, at 350°F or until light golden brown.

Nutrition: 295 Kcal, Protein 19 g, Carbs 24 g, Fat 14 g

Air Fryer Cooked Ham Tarts

Prep Time: 5 mins

Cook Time: 25 mins

Servings: 4

Ingredients:

- *Chopped fresh chives: one tbsp.*
- *Frozen puff pastry: one sheet, thawed*
- *Eggs: four large*
- *4 tbsp. cooked ham, chopped*
- *4 tbsp. of Cheddar cheese, shredded*

Instructions

Let the air fryer preheat to 400 °F

Lay puff pastry on a surface and slice into four squares.

Add two squares of puff pastry in the air fryer and cook for 8 minutes.

Take out from the air fryer and make an indentation in the dough's center. Add one tbsp. Of ham and one tbsp. Of cheddar cheese in every hole. Add one egg to it. Add on the other two squares of pastry. Seal the dough seams with water and pinch.

Return the basket to the air fryer. Let it cook to your desired doneness, for about six minutes.

Take out from the basket of the air fryer and cool for 5 minutes.

Top with chives and serve hot.

Nutrition: 153 Kcal, Protein 10 g, Carbs 7 g, Fat 7 g

Air Fried Cheesy Chicken Omelet

Prep Time: 5 mins

Cook Time: 18 mins

Servings: 2

Ingredients:

- *Cooked Chicken Breast: half cup (diced)*
- *Four eggs*

- *Onion powder: 1/4 tsp*
- *Salt: 1/2 tsp.*
- *Pepper: 1/4 tsp.*
- *Shredded cheese: 2 tbsp.*
- *Garlic powder: 1/4 tsp.*

Instructions

Take two ramekins, grease with olive oil.

Divided all ingredients in 2 portions.

Add two eggs to each ramekin. Add cheese, onion powder, salt, pepper, garlic and blend to combine. Add 1/4 cup of cooked chicken on top.

Cook at 330 °F for 14-18 minutes in the air fryer.

Nutrition: 185 Kcal, Protein 19 g, Carbs 9 g, Fat 5 g

POULTRY RECIPES

Roasted Chicken Breasts

Prep Time: 10 mins

Cook Time: 35 mins

Servings: 4

Ingredients:

- Non-stick cooking spray
- Chicken breasts (four ounces; skinless, boneless)
- Salt (optional) one tablespoon
- Black pepper Half tablespoon
- Olive oil
- One tablespoon lemon juice

- *quarter cup garlic (minced)*
- *Two tablespoons paprika*

Instructions

Heat oven to 350 degrees F. Spray a baking sheet with cooking oil. Put the chicken breasts on the baking sheet.

In a small bowl, mix salt, pepper, olive oil, lemon juice, and garlic and whisk. Pour lemon juice mixture over all pieces of chicken breast and cover each chicken breast uniformly with paprika.

Bake in the oven for 35 minutes at 165 degrees F.

Leave the chicken breasts covered with foil for ten to fifteen minutes. Then slice and serve.

Nutrition: 164 Kcal, Protein 29 g, Carbs 0 g, Fat 3.8 g

Sticky Chicken

Prep Time: 10 mins

Cook Time: 40 mins

Servings: 6

Ingredients:

- *Six chicken drumsticks*
- *Six chicken thighs*
- *Three tablespoons light soy sauce*
- *Lemon juice*
- *Six garlic cloves, finely chopped*
- *One tablespoon ginger, finely chopped*
- *Three tablespoons ground allspice*
- *One finely chopped green chili*

Instructions

Put the soy sauce, lemon juice, garlic, ginger, allspice, and chili into a large bowl. Mix well all the ingredients.

Cut the chicken and fill with marinade. Use the cling film to cover the chicken and leave in the fridge overnight.
Heat the oven to 390 degrees F.
Put the chicken in a roasting tin. Sprinkle leftover marinade.
Roast the chicken in the oven for forty minutes and take out when it gets sticky and golden.

Nutrition: 262 Kcal, Protein 42.1 g, Carbs 5.4 g, Fat 6.6 g

Turkish Marinated Chicken

Prep Time: 10 Minutes

Cook Time:15 minutes

Servings: 4

Ingredients:

- *4-6 chicken breasts, boneless, skinless*

For the marinade:

- *1 tablespoon dried oregano*
- *1 tablespoon garlic, minced*
- *1 tablespoon red wine vinegar*
- *1 teaspoon dried thyme*
- *1/2 cup lemon juice, freshly squeezed*
- *1/2 cup olive oil*

Instructions:
If there are any visible fat on the chicken, trim them off. Cut each breasts into 5-6 pieces 1-inch thick crosswise strips. Put them in a Ziploc bag or a container with tight lid.
Whisk the marinade ingredients together until combined. Pour into the bag or container with the chicken, seal, and shake the bag or the container to coat the chicken. Marinade for 6 to 8 hours or more in the refrigerator.

When marinated, remove the chicken from the fridge, let thaw to room temperature, and drain; discard the marinade. Thread the chicken strips into skewers, about 6 pieces on each skewer, the meat folded over to it would not spin around on the skewers.

Mist the grill with olive oil. Preheat the charcoal or gas grill to medium high.

Grill the skewers for about 12-15 minutes, turning once as soon as you see grill marks. Souvlaki is done when the chicken is slightly browned and firm, but not hard to the touch.

Nutrition: 360 Calories, 26 g Fat, 3 g Carbs, 30 g Protein

Chicken Broccoli Salad with Avocado Dressing

Prep Time: 5 minutes   **Cook Time: 40 minutes**
Servings: 6

Ingredients:

- *2 chicken breasts*
- *pound broccoli, cut into florets*
- *1 avocado, peeled and pitted*
- *½ lemon, juiced*
- *garlic cloves*
- *¼ teaspoon chili powder*
- *¼ teaspoon cumin powder*
- *Salt and pepper to taste*

Instructions:

Cook the chicken in a large pot of salty water.

Drain and cut the chicken into small cubes. Place in a salad bowl. Add the broccoli and mix well.

Combine the avocado, lemon juice, garlic, chili powder, cumin powder, salt and pepper in a blender. Pulse until smooth. Spoon the dressing over the salad and mix well.

Nutrition: Calories: 195; Fat: 11 g; Protein: 14 g; Carbohydrates: 3 g

Garlicky Tomato Chicken Casserole

Prep Time: 5 minutes   **Cook
Time: 50 minutes**
Servings: 4

Ingredients:

- 4 chicken breasts
- 2 tomatoes, sliced
- can diced tomatoes
- garlic cloves, chopped
- 1 shallot, chopped
- 1 bay leaf
- 1 thyme sprig
- ½ cup dry white wine
- ½ cup chicken stock
- Salt and pepper to taste

Instructions:
Combine the chicken and the remaining ingredients in a dish baking pan.
Adjust the taste with salt and pepper and cover the pot with a lid or aluminum foil.
Cook in the preheated oven at 330 °F for 40 minutes.

Nutrition: Calories: 313; Fat: 8 g, Protein: 47 g, Carbs: 6 g

Coconut Curry Chicken Tenders

Prep Time: 5 minutes   **Cook
Time: 40 minutes**
Servings: 6

Ingredients:

- 24 oz. Chicken Thighs, deboned with skin on (~5 thighs)
- 1 Egg
- 1/2 cup Pork Rinds, crumbled (~1 1/2 oz.)
- 1/2 cup Unsweetened Shredded Coconut
- 2 tsp. Curry Powder
- 1/2 tsp. Coriander
- 1/4 tsp. Garlic Powder
- 1/4 tsp. Onion Powder
- Salt and Pepper to Taste
- Sweet and Spicy Mango Dipping Sauce

Instructions:

Pre-heat oven to 400 °F. Get a cookie sheet with a wire rack ready. In a shallow bowl or plate with lips, beat an egg.

In a large resealable plastic bag, place pork rinds, coconut, and spices.

Debone chicken thighs with kitchen shears. Make sure that you leave the skin on the chicken thighs.

Cut the chicken thighs into strips (or tenders), lengthwise. This should get around 4 chicken tenders per thigh.

Dip half of the chicken into an egg and place it into the bag. Seal and shake to coat. Place chicken on wire rack. Repeat step 4 with the other half of the chicken.

Bake on the top rack in the oven for 15 minutes. Remove from the oven, flip each chicken tender, and bake for 20 minutes more.

While the chicken is cooking, prepare the sauce by mixing all of the ingredients. Set aside until the chicken is finished.

Once the chicken is ready, remove it from the oven and serve immediately.

Nutrition: 494 Calories, 34 g Fat, 1 g Carbs, 24 g Protein

Stuffed Chicken Breasts

Prep Time: 10 mins

Cook Time: 20 mins

Servings: 4

Ingredients:

- Forty-five oz boneless, skinless chicken breast cut into halves
- Four water-packed canned artichoke hearts, minced
- One tablespoon crushed dried oregano, preferably Greek
- Salt (optional)
- Freshly ground pepper
- One tsp olive oil
- One cup fat-free unsalted canned chicken broth
- One-fourth cup plus half tablespoon fresh lemon juice
- Four slices of lemon
- Two tablespoons cornstarch
- Chopped parsley for garnish

Instructions

Remove any obvious chicken fat, rinse it and pat it dry. Season the chicken with salt and pepper.

Place the halves with the flat side of a meat mallet between 2 pieces of plastic wrap and pound until the chicken is very thin and flat.

Mix the heart of the artichoke and oregano. Put equal amounts of the artichoke mixture into the middle of each pounded chicken breast. Just roll up with a toothpick or skewer, secure.

Heat the oil over low heat in a non-stick pan. On both ends, add chicken and brown equally. Pour on the lemon juice and broth.

Cover chicken with lemon slices, and boil (about 15 to 20 minutes) until chicken is cooked through.

Shift chicken, discarding toothpicks/skewers, to a tray. Keep warm.

Mix cornstarch with the remaining 1 1/2 tsp of lemon juice using a fork. Apply to a skillet and whisk until slightly thickened, over high fire.

Spoon the chicken with lemon sauce. Garnish with parsley and lemon slices.

Nutrition: 189 Kcal, Protein 25 g, Carbs 5.9 g, Fat 6.8 g

Low-Fat Baked Chicken

Prep Time: 5 mins

Cook Time: 20 mins

Servings: 4

Ingredients:

- *Sixteen oz boneless skinless chicken breasts*
- *Half cup breadcrumbs*
- *One-fourth cup fat-free parmesan cheese*
- *One tablespoon rosemary*
- *One tablespoon basil*
- *Half tablespoon oregano*
- *One tablespoon black pepper*
- *One tablespoon parsley flakes*
- *One-third cup olive oil*

Instructions
Heat oven to 375 degrees F.
Combine bread crumbs, cheese, rosemary, basil, oregano, pepper, and parsley in a bowl.
Put each chicken breast in olive oil and in bread crumb mixture.
Put each breast on a baking sheet and bake for about twenty to thirty minutes or until golden brown.

Nutrition: 174 Kcal, Protein 24.3 g, Carbs 7.8 g, Fat 4.3 g

Orange Chicken

Prep Time: 15 mins

Cook Time: 15 mins

Servings: 4

Ingredients:

- *Four pieces of boneless skinless breast cut into halves*
- *Two tablespoons olive oil*
- *Two cups of water*
- *One tablespoon Corn starch*
- *One container Wal-Mart Sugar-Free Drink Mix*

Instructions

Clean and cut any extra fat from the chicken and slice into bite-sized parts.

In a covered skillet or electric oven, put the chicken, oil, and drink mix.

Cook for 15 to 20 minutes on low heat.

Meanwhile, dissolve limited quantities of water with corn starch. Stir in the orange sauce and boil until the mixture thickens. Insert the chicken and stir until it's covered.

Nutrition: 140 Kcal, Protein 23 g, Carbs 0.8 g, Fat 2.9 g

Chicken Salad with Walnuts

Prep Time: 15 mins

Cook Time: 15 mins

Servings: 4

Ingredients:

- *Five pounds skinless, boneless chicken breasts*
- *Three fourth cup non-fat sour cream*
- *Three fourth cup non-fat mayonnaise*

- *Two tablespoons white wine vinegar*
- *Four celery ribs, cut into small dice*
- *Half cup walnuts*
- *One-quarter cup chopped fresh tarragon*
- *Freshly ground pepper*
- *One tablespoon salt*
- *Extra tarragon for garnish*

Instructions

Poach the chicken breasts in a simmering broth for about 15 minutes before cooking through. Drain, cool, and slice (or shred) into parts that are bite-sized.
Mix the sour cream, mayonnaise, and vinegar in a shallow tub.
Mix the dressing and chicken.
Add the celery, walnuts, tarragon, and pepper to taste prior to eating.

Nutrition: 255 Kcal, Protein 18.4 g, Carbs 6.1 g, Fat 4.9 g

Asian Soup with Shredded Chicken

Prep Time: 10 mins

Cook Time: 40 mins

Servings: 4

Ingredients:

- *Four dried black mushrooms, rinsed*
- *One large clove garlic, minced*
- *One small Serrano or Thai chili pepper, seeded and minced*
- *One tablespoon minced fresh ginger*
- *Six cups low-sodium canned chicken broth*
- *Two tablespoons low-sodium soy sauce*
- *Twenty-six oz chicken breast halves, poached and shredded*
- *Four4 oz trimmed snow peas*
- *One small carrot, two oz thinly sliced*

- *Two fresh water chestnuts, peeled and thinly sliced. You can also use canned chestnuts*
- *Four thinly sliced scallions*
- *salt to taste*
- *fresh ground pepper to taste*

Instructions

Mix mushrooms, garlic, chili pepper, ginger, chicken broth, and soy sauce in a pot of soup. Boil it at a moderate temperature for 2 minutes. Remove it from the stove, cover, and keep it for 30 minutes.

Use a slotted spoon for removing black mushrooms. Then slice. Transfer to the pot.

Boil the mixture again. Add leftover ingredients with the exception of scallions.

Reduce the heat and simmer for 10 minutes.

Add scallions, stir and pour soup into normal soup bowls.

Then serve immediately.

Nutrition: 202 Kcal, Protein 16.1 g, Carbs 11.2 g, Fat 0.9 g

Sausage Strata

Prep Time: 20 mins

   Cook Time: 1 hour

Servings: 8

Ingredients:

- *Cooking spray*
- *One lb. chicken sausages*
- *Two cups of milk*
- *One and a half cup egg substitute*
- *Three-quarters shredded low-fat cheddar cheese*
- *Eight slices whole grain bread. Remove crusts and cut into cubes*

- *One and a half cup of roasted tomatillo salsa*

Instructions

Remove and discard casings of sausage. Crumble the sausage and sauté over medium heat in a non-stick pan until uniformly browned, stirring and using a wooden spoon to break up any big clumps. Move the browned sausage to a plate filled with paper towels to drain properly by using a slotted spoon.

Stir together the milk and egg replacement in a one-quart mixing cup. Cover a two-quart casserole platter lightly with cooking oil. Place a quarter cup of shredded cheese in a plastic bag for self-sealing. And refrigerate. (You will save this when you bake it, to sprinkle on top.) Layer the bottom of the casserole dish with one-third of the bread cubes. Add half of the browned sausage and a fourth of the melted cheese to the top. Pour over the top one cup of the milk-egg mixture.

The layers are repeated (one-third of the bread, the rest of the sausage, a quarter of a cup of shredded cheese).

Put on the rest of the bread for the last layer and then dump over the remaining one and a half cup of the milk-egg mixture. Cover with salsa of tomatillo.

Cover overnight with plastic wrap and refrigerate.

Heat the oven to 350 ° F, open the casserole, and sprinkle the surface with the reserved shredded cheese. Bake for about 50 to 60 minutes until the strata start to bubble and turn golden brown. The inserted knife must come out easily.

Remove from the oven and let it remain there for additional ten minutes. Then serve instantly.

Nutrition: 367 Kcal, Protein 22.3 g, Carbs 13.5 g, Fat 25.3 g

Oven Parmesan Chicken

Prep Time: 15 mins

      Cook Time: 1 hour 10 mins

Servings: 6

Ingredients:

- *One clove crushed garlic*
- *One-quarter lb. butter, melted*
- *One cup dried bread crumbs*
- *One-third cup grated Parmesan cheese*
- *Two tablespoons chopped fresh parsley*
- *1 tsp salt*
- *Pinch of ground black pepper*
- *Four lb. chicken, cut into pieces*

Instructions

Heat oven to 350 degrees F.

Mix the crushed garlic with the melted butter in a bowl or a dish. Combine together the bread crumbs, cheese, parsley, salt, and pepper in a bowl. Put chicken pieces into garlic butter. Then cover it with crumb mixture.

Put coated chicken pieces into a moderately greased 9x13 inch baking dish. Sprinkle remaining garlic butter.

Bake uncovered in the preheated oven for another one and a quarter of hours. Bake till chicken is cooked through, and juices become visible.

Nutrition: 587 Kcal, Protein 43.2 g, Carbs 13.4 g, Fat 37.4 g

Herbed Roasted Chicken Breasts

Prep Time: 5 minutes minutes   **Cook Time: 50**

Servings: 4

Ingredients:

- 2 tablespoons extra virgin olive oil
- 2 tablespoons chopped parsley
- 2 tablespoons chopped cilantro
- teaspoon dried oregano
- 1 teaspoon dried basil
- tablespoons lemon juice
- Salt and pepper to taste
- chicken breasts

Instructions:

Combine the oil, parsley, cilantro, oregano, basil, lemon juice, salt and pepper in a bowl.

Spread this mixture over the chicken and rub it well into the meat.

Place in a dish baking pan and cover with aluminum foil.

Cook in the preheated oven at 350F for 20 minutes then remove the foil and cook for 25 additional minutes.

Serve the chicken warm and fresh with your favorite side dish.

Nutrition: Calories: 330; Fat: 15 g; Protein: 40.7 g; Carbohydrates: 1 g

Chicken and Cashew Salad

Prep Time: 15 mins

Servings: 1

Ingredients:

- One small cooked and shredded skinless chicken breast
- One peeled and shredded carrot
- A handful of trimmed and sliced green beans
- One quarter shredded white or red cabbage
- One finely sliced shallot

- *A handful of watercress*
- *Two tablespoons toasted cashew nuts*
- *One tablespoon toasted sesame seeds*
- *One tablespoon lime juice*
- *One tablespoon soy sauce*
- *chives chopped*
- *One tablespoon rice vinegar*

Instructions:

Combine together the dressing ingredients (lime juice, soy sauce, chives, rice vinegar). Mix with one tablespoon of water. Put the carrot, chicken, green beans, cabbage, shallot, and the dressings in a bowl. Add the watercress before serving. Cut the cashews and put them into the bowl. Cover with sesame seeds before serving.

Nutrition: 487 Kcal, Protein 40.7 g, Carbs 19.7 g, Fat 22.8 g, Sugars 13 g

Chicken & Veggie Kabobs

Prep Time: 20 minutes   **Cook Time: 10 minutes**
Servings: 8

Ingredients:

- *¼ cup white vinegar*
- *¼ cup fresh lemon juice*
- *¼ cup olive oil*
- *2 garlic cloves, minced*
- *½ teaspoon dried thyme, crushed*
- *½ teaspoon dried oregano, crushed*
- *1 teaspoon ground cumin*
- *Salt and ground black pepper, as required*
- *2 pounds skinless, boneless chicken breast, cubed into ½-inch size*
- *1 large orange bell pepper, seeded and cubed into 1-inch size*
- *1 large green bell pepper, seeded and cubed into 1-inch size*

- *16 fresh mushrooms*
- *16 cherry tomatoes*
- *1 large red onion, quartered and separated into pieces*

Instructions:
In a large bowl, add the vinegar, lemon juice, oil, garlic, dried herbs, cumin, salt and black pepper and mix until well combined.
Add the chicken cubes and coat with mixture generously.
Refrigerate, covered to marinate for about 2-4 hours.
Preheat the outdoor grill to medium-high heat. Grease the grill grate.
Remove the chicken from the bowl and discard the excess marinade.
Thread the chicken and vegetables onto pre-soaked wooden skewers respectively.
Grill for about 10 minutes, flipping occasionally or until desired doneness.

Nutrition: Calories 232, Fat 10.7 g, Carbs 7.1 g, Sugar 4 g, Protein 27.4 g

Chicken with Caper Sauce

Prep Time: 20 minutes   **Cook Time: 18 minutes**
Servings: 5

Ingredients:

For Chicken:

- *2 eggs*
- *Salt and ground black pepper, as required*
- *1 cup dry breadcrumbs*
- *2 tablespoons olive oil*
- *1½ pounds skinless, boneless chicken breast halves, pounded into ¾-inch thickness and cut into pieces*

For Capers Sauce:

- 3 tablespoons capers
- ½ cup dry white wine
- 3 tablespoons fresh lemon juice
- Salt and ground black pepper, as required
- 2 tablespoons fresh parsley, chopped

Instructions:

For chicken: in a shallow dish, add the eggs, salt and black pepper and beat until well combined.

In another shallow dish, place breadcrumbs.

Dip the chicken pieces in egg mixture then coat with the breadcrumbs evenly.

In a large skillet, heat the oil over medium heat and cook the chicken pieces for about 5-7 minutes per side or until desired doneness.

With a slotted spoon, transfer the chicken pieces onto a paper towel-lined plate.

With a piece of the foil, cover the chicken pieces to keep them warm.

In the same skillet, add all the sauce ingredients except parsley and cook for about 2-3 minutes, stirring continuously. Stir in the parsley and remove from heat.

Serve the chicken pieces with the topping of capers sauce.

Nutrition: Calories 352, Fat 13.5 g, Carbs 16.9 g, Sugar 1.9 g, Protein 35.7 g

Grilled Chicken Breasts

Prep Time: 15 minutes   **Cook Time: 12 minutes**
Servings: 4

Ingredients:

- *4 (4-ounce) boneless, skinless chicken breast halves*
- *3 garlic cloves, chopped finely*
- *3 tablespoons fresh parsley, chopped*
- *3 tablespoons olive oil*
- *3 tablespoons lemon juice*
- *1 teaspoon paprika*
- *½ teaspoon dried oregano*
- *Salt and ground black pepper, as required*

Instructions:

With a fork, pierce chicken breasts several times

In a large bowl, add all the ingredients except the chicken breasts and mix until well combined. Add the chicken breasts and coat with the marinade generously.

Refrigerate to marinate for about 2-3 hours.

Preheat the grill to medium-high heat. Grease the grill grate.

Remove chicken from marinade and grill for about 5-6 minutes per side.

Nutrition: Calories 315, Fat 19.1, Carbs 1.6 g, Sugar 0.3 g, Protein 33.2 g

AIR-FRY RECIPES

Turkey Fajitas Platter in Air Fryer

Prep Time: 5 mins

  Cook Time: 20 mins

Servings: 2

Ingredients:

- *Cooked Turkey Breast: 1/4 cup*
- *Six Tortilla Wraps*
- *One Avocado*
- *One Yellow Pepper*
- *One Red Pepper*
- *Half Red Onion*
- *Soft Cheese: 5 Tbsp.*
- *Mexican Seasoning: 2 Tbsp.*
- *Cumin: 1 Tsp*
- *Kosher salt& Pepper*
- *Cajun Spice: 3 Tbsp.*
- *Fresh Coriander*

Instructions:
Chop up the avocado and slice the vegetables.
Dice up turkey breast into small bite-size pieces.
In a bowl, add onions, turkey, soft cheese, and peppers along with seasonings. Mix it well.
Place it in foil and the air fryer.
Cook for 20 minutes at 392 °F.
Serve hot.

Nutritional: 379 kcal, Protein 30 g, Carbs 64 g, Fat 29 g

Turkey Juicy Breast Tenderloin

Prep Time: 5 mins

Cook Time: 25 mins

Servings: 3

Ingredients:

- *Turkey breast tenderloin: one-piece*
- *Thyme: half tsp.*
- *Sage: half tsp.*
- *Paprika: half tsp.*
- *Pink salt: half tsp.*
- *Freshly ground black pepper: half tsp.*

Instructions

Let the air fryer preheat to 350 °F

In a bowl, mix all the spices and herbs, rub it all over the turkey. Spray oil on the air fryer basket. Put the turkey in the air fryer and let it cook at 350 F for 25 minutes, flip halfway through. Serve with your favorite salad.

Nutritional: 162 Kcal, Protein 13 g, Carbs 1 g, Fat 1 g

Turkey Breast with Mustard Glaze

Prep Time: 10 mins

Cook Time: 56 mins

Servings: 6

Ingredients:

- *Whole turkey breast: 5 pounds*
- *Olive oil: 2 tsp.*
- *Dried sage: half tsp.*
- *Smoked paprika: half tsp.*
- *Dried thyme: one tsp.*
- *Salt: one tsp.*
- *Freshly ground black pepper: half tsp.*
- *Dijon mustard: 2 tbsp.*

Instructions:

Let the air fryer preheat to 350 ° F

Rub the olive oil all over the turkey breast.

In a bowl, mix salt, sage, pepper, thyme, and paprika. Mix well and coat turkey in this spice rub.

Place the turkey in an air fryer, cook for 25 minutes at 350ºF. Flip the turkey over and cook for another 12 minutes. Flip again and cook for another ten minutes. With an instant-read thermometer, the internal temperature should reach 165ºF.

In the meantime, in a saucepan, mix mustard and with one tsp. of butter.

Brush this glaze all over the turkey when cooked.

Cook again for five minutes.

Nutritional value: 379 Kcal, Carbs 21 g, Protein 52 g, Fat 23 g

Zucchini Turkey Burgers

Prep Time: 10 mins

        Cook Time: 10 mins

Servings: 5

Ingredients:

- *Gluten-free breadcrumbs: 1/4 cup (seasoned)*

- *Grated zucchini: 1 cup*
- *Red onion: 1 tbsp. (grated)*
- *Lean ground turkey: 4 cups*
- *One clove of minced garlic*
- *1 tsp of kosher salt and fresh pepper*

Instructions:

In a bowl, add zucchini (moisture removed with a paper towel), ground turkey, garlic, salt, onion, pepper, breadcrumbs. Mix well.
With your hands make five patties. But not too thick.
Let the air fryer preheat to 375 F
Put in an air fryer in a single layer and cook for 7 minutes or more. Until cooked through and browned.
Place in buns with ketchup and lettuce and enjoy.

Nutritional value: 161 Kcal, Carbs 4.5 g, Protein 18 g, Fat 7 g

No-breaded Turkey Breast

Prep Time: 5 mins

Cook Time: 55 mins

Servings: 10

Ingredients:

a. *Turkey breast: 4 pounds, ribs removed, bone with skin*
b. *Olive oil: 1 tablespoon*
c. *Salt: 2 teaspoons*
d. *Dry turkey seasoning (without salt): half tsp.*

Instructions:

Rub half tbsp of olive oil over turkey breast. Sprinkle salt, turkey seasoning on both sides of turkey breast with half tbsp of olive oil.

Let the air fryer preheat at 350 F. put turkey skin side down in air fryer and cook for 20 minutes until the turkey's temperature reaches 160 F for half an hour to 40 minutes.
Let it sit for ten minutes before slicing.
Serve with fresh salad.

Nutritional value: 226 kcal, Carbs 22 g, Protein 32.5 g, Fat 10 g

Breaded Chicken Tenderloins

Prep Time: 10 mins
              Cook Time: 12 mins
Servings: 4

Ingredients:

- *Eight chicken tenderloins*
- *Olive oil: 2 tablespoons*
- *One egg whisked*
- *1/4 cup breadcrumbs*

Instructions:
Let the air fryer heat to 356F.
In a big bowl, add breadcrumbs and oil, mix well until forms a crumbly mixture
Dip chicken tenderloin in whisked egg and coat in breadcrumbs mixture.
Place the breaded chicken in the air fryer and cook at 180C for 12 minutes or more.
Take out from the air fryer and serve with your favorite green salad.

Nutrition: 206kcal, Proteins 20g, Carbs 17g, Fat 10g

Parmesan Chicken Meatballs

Prep Time: 10 mins

           Cook Time: 12 mins

Servings: 20

Ingredients:

- *Pork rinds: half cup, ground*
- *Ground chicken: 4 cups*
- *Parmesan cheese: half cup grated*
- *Kosher salt: 1 tsp.*
- *Garlic powder: 1/2 tsp.*
- *One egg beaten*
- *Paprika: 1/2 tsp.*
- *Pepper: half tsp.*

Breading:

- *Whole wheat breadcrumbs: half cup ground*

Instructions:

Let the Air Fryer pre-heat to 400°F.

Add cheese, chicken, egg, pepper, half cup of pork rinds, garlic, salt, and paprika in a big mixing ball. Mix well into a dough, make into 1and half-inch balls.

Coat the meatballs in whole wheat bread crumbs.

Spray the oil in the air fry basket and add meatballs in one even layer.

Let it cook for 12 minutes at 400°F, flipping once halfway through.

Serve with salad greens.

Nutrition: 240kcal, protein 19.9 g, Carbs 12.1 g, Fat 10 g

Lemon Rosemary Chicken

Prep Time: 30 mins

Cook Time: 20 mins

Servings: 2

Ingredients:
For marinade:

- *Chicken: 2 and ½ cups*
- *Ginger: 1 tsp, minced*
- *Olive oil: 1/2 tbsp.*
- *Soy sauce: 1 tbsp.*

For the sauce:

- *Half lemon*
- *Honey: 3 tbsp.*
- *Oyster sauce: 1 tbsp.*
- *Fresh rosemary: half cup, chopped*

Instructions:
In a big mixing bowl, add the marinade ingredients with chicken, and mix well.

Keep in the refrigerator for at least half an hour.

Let the oven preheat to 392F for three minutes.

Place the marinated chicken in the air fryer in a single layer. And cook for 6 minutes at 392F.

Meanwhile, add all the sauces ingredients in a bowl and mix well except for lemon wedges.

Brush the sauce generously over half-baked chicken add lemon juice on top.

Cook for another 13 minutes at 392F. flip the chicken halfway through. Let the chicken evenly brown.

Serve right away and enjoy.

Nutrition: 308kcal, Proteins 25g, Carbs 7g, Fat 12 g

Air Fryer Chicken & Broccoli

Prep Time: 10 mins

Cook Time: 15 mins

Servings: 4

Ingredients:

- *Olive oil: 2 Tablespoons*
- *Chicken breast: 4 cups, bone and skinless (cut into cubes)*
- *Half medium onion, roughly sliced*
- *Low sodium soy sauce: 1 Tbsp.*
- *Garlic powder: half teaspoon*
- *Rice vinegar: 2 teaspoons*
- *Broccoli: 1-2 cups, cut into florets*
- *Hot sauce: 2 teaspoons*
- *Fresh minced ginger: 1 Tbsp.*
- *Sesame seed oil: 1 teaspoon*
- *Salt & black pepper, to taste*

Instructions:

In a bowl, add chicken breast, onion, and broccoli. Combine them well.

In another bowl, add ginger, oil, sesame oil, rice vinegar, hot sauce, garlic powder, and soy sauce mix it well. Then add the broccoli, chicken, and onions to marinade.

Coat well the chicken with sauces. And let it rest in the refrigerator for 15 minutes

Place chicken mix in one even layer in air fryer basket and cook for 16-20 minutes, at 380 F. halfway through, toss the basket gently and

cook the chicken evenly
Add five minutes more, if required.
Add salt and pepper, if needed.
Serve hot with lemon wedges.

Nutrition: 191kcal, Protein 25g, Carbohydrates 4g, Fat 7g

Air Fried Maple Chicken Thighs

Prep Time: 10
mins
             Cook Time: 25 mins
Servings: 4

Ingredients:

- *One egg*
- *Buttermilk: 1 cup*
- *Maple syrup: half cup*
- *Chicken thighs: 4 pieces*
- *Granulated garlic: 1 tsp.*

Dry Mix:

- *Granulated garlic: half tsp.*
- *All-purpose flour: half cup*
- *Salt: one tbsp.*
- *Sweet paprika: one tsp.*
- *Smoked paprika: half tsp.*
- *Tapioca flour: ¼ cup*
- *Cayenne pepper: ¼ teaspoon*
- *Granulated onion: one tsp.*
- *Black pepper: ¼ teaspoon*
- *Honey powder: half tsp.*

Instructions:

In a ziploc bag, add egg, one tsp. of granulated garlic, buttermilk, and maple syrup, add in the chicken thighs and let it marinate for one hour or more in the refrigerator

In a mixing bowl, add sweet paprika, tapioca flour, granulated onion, half tsp. of granulated garlic, flour, cayenne pepper, salt, pepper, honey powder, and smoked paprika mix it well.

Let the air fry preheat to 380 F

Coat the marinated chicken thighs in the dry spice mix, shake the excess off.

Put the chicken skin side down in the air fryer

Let it cook for 12 minutes. Flip thighs halfway through and cook for 13 minutes more.

Serve with salad greens.

Nutrition: 415.4 kcal, Protein 23.3g, Carbs 20.8g, Fat 13.4g

Mushroom Oatmeal

Prep Time: 10 mins
       Cook Time: 20 mins
Servings: 4

Ingredients:

- One small yellow onion, chopped
- 1 cup steel-cut oats
- 1 Garlic cloves, minced
- 2 Tablespoons butter
- ½ cup of water
- One and a half cup of canned chicken stock
- Thyme springs, chopped
- 2 Tablespoons extra virgin olive oil
- ½ cup gouda cheese, grated
- 1 cup mushroom, sliced

- Salt and black pepper to taste

Instructions:

Heat a pan over medium heat, which suits your air fryer with the butter, add onions and garlic, stir and cook for 4 minutes.

Add oats, sugar, salt, pepper, stock, and thyme, stir, place in the air fryer and cook for 16 minutes at 360 F.

In the meantime, prepare a skillet over medium heat with the olive oil, add mushrooms, cook them for 3 minutes, add oatmeal and cheese, whisk, divide into bowls and serve for breakfast.

Enjoy.

Nutrition: 284kcal, Protein 17g, Carbs 20g, Fat 8g

Bell Peppers Frittata

Prep Time: 10 mins
                    Cook Time: 20 mins
Servings: 4

Ingredients:

- 2 Tablespoons olive oil
- 2 cups chicken sausage, casings removed and chopped
- One sweet onion, chopped
- 1 red bell pepper, chopped
- 1 orange bell pepper, chopped
- 1 green bell pepper, chopped
- Salt and black pepper to taste
- 8 eggs, whisked
- ½ cup mozzarella cheese, shredded
- 2 teaspoons oregano, chopped

Instructions:

Add 1 spoonful of oil to the air fryer, add bacon, heat to 320 F, and brown for 1 minute.

Remove remaining butter, onion, red bell pepper, orange and white, mix and simmer for another 2 minutes.

Stir and cook for 15 minutes, add oregano, salt, pepper, and eggs.

Add mozzarella, leave frittata aside for a couple of minutes, divide and serve between plates.

Enjoy.

Nutrition: 212kcal, Protein 12g, Carbs 8g, Fat 4g

Southwest Chicken in Air Fryer

Prep Time: 20 mins

Cook Time: 30 mins

Servings: 4

Ingredients:

- *Avocado oil: one tbsp.*
- *Four cups of boneless, skinless, chicken breast*
- *Chili powder: half tsp.*
- *Salt to taste*
- *Cumin: half tsp.*
- *Onion powder: 1/4 tsp.*
- *Lime juice: two tbsp.*
- *Garlic powder: 1/4 tsp*

Instructions:

In a ziploc bag, add chicken, oil, and lime juice.

Add all spices in a bowl and rub all over the chicken in the ziploc bag.

Let it marinate in the fridge for ten minutes or more.

Take chicken out from the ziploc bag and put it in the air fryer.

Cook for 25 minutes at 400 F, flipping chicken halfway through until internal temperature reaches 165 degrees.

Nutrition: 165kcal, Protein: 24g, Carbs 1g, Fat 6g

No-Breading Chicken Breast in Air Fryer

Prep Time: 10 mins
                Cook Time: 20 mins
Servings: 2

Ingredients:

- *Olive oil spray*
- *Chicken breasts: 4 (boneless)*
- *Onion powder: 3/4 teaspoon*
- *Salt: ¼ cup*
- *Smoked paprika: half tsp.*
- *1/8 tsp. of cayenne pepper*
- *Garlic powder: 3/4 teaspoon*
- *Dried parsley: half tsp.*

Instructions:

In a large bowl, add six cups of warm water, add salt (1/4 cup) and mix to dissolve.

Put chicken breasts in the warm salted water and let it refrigerate for almost 2 hours.

Remove from water and pat dry.

In a bowl, add all the spices with ¾ tsp. of salt. Spray the oil all over the chicken and rub the spice mix all over the chicken.

Let the air fryer heat at 380F.

Put the chicken in the air fryer and cook for ten minutes. Flip halfway through and serve with salad green.

Nutrition: 208kcal, Protein 39g, Carbs 1g, Fat 4.5g

Lemon Pepper Chicken Breast

Prep Time: 3 mins
Cook Time: 15 mins
Servings: 2

Ingredients:

- *Two Lemons rind, juice, and zest*
- *One Chicken Breast*
- *Minced Garlic: 1 Tsp*
- *Black Peppercorns: 2 tbsp.*
- *Chicken Seasoning: 1 Tbsp.*
- *Salt & pepper, to taste*

Instructions
Let the air fryer preheat to 356F.
In a large aluminum foil, add all the seasonings along with lemon rind.
Add salt and pepper to chicken and rub the seasonings all over chicken breast.
Put the chicken in aluminum foil. And fold it tightly.
Flatten the chicken inside foil with a rolling pin
Put it in the air fryer and cook at 356F for 15 minutes.
Serve hot.

Nutrition: 140kcal, Protein 13g, Carbs 24g, Fat 2g

Herb-Marinated Chicken Thighs

Prep Time: 30 mins

        Cook Time: 10 mins

Servings: 4

Ingredients:

- *Chicken thighs: 8 skin-on, bone-in,*
- *Lemon juice: 2 Tablespoon*
- *Onion powder: half teaspoon*
- *Garlic powder: 2 teaspoon*
- *Spike Seasoning: 1 teaspoon.*
- *Olive oil: 1/4 cup*
- *Dried basil: 1 teaspoon*
- *Dried oregano: half teaspoon.*
- *Black Pepper: 1/4 tsp.*

Instructions:

In a bowl, add dried oregano, olive oil, lemon juice, dried sage, garlic powder, Spike Seasoning, onion powder, dried basil, black pepper.

In a ziploc bag, add the spice blend and the chicken and mix well.

Marinate the chicken in the refrigerator for at least six hours or more.

Preheat the air fryer to 360F.

Put the chicken in the air fryer basket, cook for six-eight minutes, flip the chicken, and cook for six minutes more.

Until the internal chicken temperature reaches 165F.

Take out from the air fryer and serve with microgreens.

Nutrition: 100kcal, Protein 4g, Carbs 1g, Fat 9g

Air Fried Chicken Fajitas

Prep Time: 10 mins

        Cook Time: 20 mins

Servings: 6

Ingredients:

- *Chicken breasts: 4 cups, cut into thin strips*
- *Bell peppers, sliced*
- *Salt: half tsp.*
- *Cumin: 1 tsp.*
- *Garlic powder: 1/4 tsp*
- *Chili powder: half tsp.*
- *Lime juice: 1 tbsp.*

Instructions:
In a bowl, add seasonings, chicken and lime juice, and mix well.
Then add sliced peppers and coat well.
Spray the air fryer with olive oil.
Put the chicken and peppers in, and cook for 15 minutes at 400 F.
Flip halfway through.
Serve with wedges of lemons and enjoy.

Nutrition: 140kcal, Proteins 22g, Carbs 6g, Fat 5g

Air Fried Blackened Chicken Breast

Prep Time: 10 mins

    Cook Time: 20 mins

Servings: 2

Ingredients:

- *Paprika: 2 teaspoons*
- *Ground thyme: 1 teaspoon*
- *Cumin: 1 teaspoon*
- *Cayenne pepper: half tsp.*
- *Onion powder: half tsp.*

- *Black Pepper: half tsp.*
- *Salt: ¼ teaspoon*
- *Vegetable oil: 2 teaspoons*
- *Pieces of chicken breast halves (without bones and skin)*

Instructions:

In a mixing bowl, add onion powder, salt, cumin, paprika, black pepper, thyme, and cayenne pepper. Mix it well.

Drizzle oil over chicken and rub. Dip each piece of chicken in blackening spice blend on both sides.

Let it rest for five minutes while the air fryer is preheating.

Preheat it for five minutes at 360F.

Put the chicken in the air fryer and let it cook for ten minutes. Flip and then cook for another ten minutes.

After, let it sit for five minutes, then slice and serve with the side of greens.

Nutrition: 432.1kcal, Protein 79.4g, Carbs 3.2g, Fat 9.5g

Chicken with Mixed Vegetables

Prep Time: 10 mins

Cook Time: 20 mins

Servings: 2

Ingredients:

- *1/2 onion diced*
- *Chicken breast: 4 cups, cubed pieces*
- *Half zucchini chopped*
- *Italian seasoning: 1 tablespoon*
- *Bell pepper chopped: 1/2 cup*
- *Clove of garlic pressed*
- *Broccoli florets: 1/2 cup*

- *Olive oil: 2 tablespoons*
- *Half teaspoon of chili powder, garlic powder, pepper, salt*

Instructions:

Let the air fryer heat to 400 F and dice the vegetables

In a bowl, add the seasoning, oil and add vegetables, chicken and toss well

Place chicken and vegetables in the air fryer, and cook for ten minutes, toss half way through, cook in batches.

Make sure the veggies are charred and the chicken is cooked through.

Serve hot.

Nutrition: 230kcal, Protein 26g, Carbs 8g, Fat 10g

Garlic Parmesan Chicken Tenders

Prep Time: 5 mins

Cook Time: 12 mins

Servings: 4

Ingredients:

- *One egg*
- *Eight raw chicken tenders*
- *Water: 2 tablespoons*
- *Olive oil*

To coat:

- *Panko breadcrumbs: 1 cup*
- *Half tsp of salt*
- *Black Pepper: 1/4 teaspoon*
- *Garlic powder: 1 teaspoon*

- *Onion powder: 1/2 teaspoon*
- *Parmesan cheese: 1/4 cup*
- *Any dipping Sauc*

Instructions:
Add all the coating ingredients in a big bowl
In another bowl, mix water and egg.
Dip the chicken in the egg mix, then in the coating mix.
Put the tenders in the air fry basket in a single layer.
Spray with the olive oil light
Cook at 400 degrees for 12 minutes. Flip the chicken halfway through.
Serve with salad greens and enjoy.

Nutrition: 220kcal, Protein 27g, Carbs 13g, Fat 6g

Chicken Thighs Smothered Style

Prep Time: 30 mins
        Cook Time: 30 mins
Servings: 4

Ingredients:

- *8-ounce of chicken thighs*
- *1 tsp paprika*
- *One pinch salt*
- *Mushrooms: half cup*
- *Onions, roughly sliced*

Instructions:
Let the air fryer preheat to 400F
Chicken thighs season with paprika, salt, and pepper on both sides.
Place the thighs in the air fryer and cook for 20 minutes.

Meanwhile, sauté the mushroom and onion.
Take out the thighs from the air fryer serve with sautéed mushrooms and onions.
And serve with chopped scallions and on the side of salad greens

Nutrition: 466.3kcal, Protein 40.5g, Carbs 2.4g, Fat 32g

Lemon-Garlic Chicken

Prep Time: 2 hours

Cook Time: 35 mins

Servings: 4

Ingredients:

- *Lemon juice ¼ cup*
- *1 Tbsp. olive oil*
- *1 tsp mustard*
- *Cloves of garlic*
- *¼ tsp salt*
- *⅛ tsp black pepper*
- *Chicken thighs*
- *Lemon wedges*

Instructions:

In a bowl, whisk together the olive oil, lemon juice, mustard Dijon, garlic, salt, and pepper.
Place the chicken thighs in a large ziploc bag. Spill marinade over chicken & seal bag, ensuring all chicken parts are covered. Cool for at least 2 hours.
Preheat a frying pan to 360 F.
Remove the chicken with towels from the marinade, & pat dry.
Place pieces of chicken in the air fryer basket, if necessary, cook them in batches.

Fry till chicken is no longer pink on the bone & the juices run smoothly, 22 to 24 min. Upon serving, press a lemon slice across each piece.

Nutrition: 258kcal, Protein: 19.4g, Carbs 3.6g, Fat 18.6g

Buttermilk Chicken in Air-Fryer

Prep Time: 30 mins
                    Cook Time: 20 mins

Servings: 6

Ingredients:

- *Chicken thighs: 4 cups skin-on, bone-in*

Marinade:

- *Buttermilk: 2 cups*
- *Black pepper: 2 tsp.*
- *Cayenne pepper: 1 tsp.*
- *Salt: 2 tsp.*

Seasoned Flour:

- *Baking powder: 1 tbsp.*
- *All-purpose flour: 2 cups*
- *Paprika powder: 1 tbsp.*
- *Salt: 1 tsp.*
- *Garlic powder: 1 tbsp.*

Instructions:
Let the air fry heat at 356F.
With a paper towel, pat dry the chicken thighs.

In a mixing bowl, add paprika, black pepper, salt mix well, then add chicken pieces. Add buttermilk and coat the chicken well. Let it marinate for at least 6 hours.

In another bowl, add baking powder, salt, flour, pepper, and paprika. Put one by one of the chicken pieces and coat in the seasoning mix. Spray oil on chicken pieces and place breaded chicken skin side up in air fryer basket in one layer, cook for 8 minutes, then flip the chicken pieces' cook for another ten minutes

Take out from the air fryer and serve right away.

Nutrition: 210kcal, Protein 22g, Carbs 12 g, Fat 18 g

Orange Chicken Wings

Prep Time: 5 mins

Cook Time: 14 mins

Servings: 2

Ingredients:

- *Chicken Wings, Six pieces*
- *One orange zest and juice*
- *Worcestershire Sauce: 1.5 tbsp.*
- *Black pepper to taste*
- *Herbs (sage, rosemary, oregano, parsley, basil, thyme, and mint)*

Instructions:
Wash and pat dry the chicken wings

In a bowl, add chicken wings, pour zest and orange juice

Add the rest of the ingredients and rub on chicken wings. Let it marinate for at least half an hour.

Let the Air fryer preheat at 356F.

In an aluminum foil, wrap the marinated wings and put them in an air fryer, and cook for 20 minutes at 356F.

After 20 minutes, remove aluminum foil and brush the sauce over wings and cook for 15 minutes more. Then again, brush the sauce and cook for another ten minutes.

Take out from the air fryer and serve hot.

Nutrition: 271kcal, Protein 29g, Carbs 20g, Fat 15g

Air Fryer Brown Rice Chicken Fried

Prep Time: 10 mins

Cook Time: 20 mins

Servings: 2

Ingredients:

- *Olive Oil Cooking Spray*
- *Chicken Breast: 1 Cup, Diced & Cooked &*
- *White Onion: 1/4 cup chopped*
- *Celery: 1/4 Cup chopped*
- *Cooked brown rice: 4 Cups*
- *Carrots: 1/4 cup chopped*

Instructions:

Place foil on the air fryer basket, make sure to leave room for air to flow, roll up on the sides.

Spray with olive oil, the foil. Mix all ingredients.

On top of the foil, add all ingredients in the air fryer basket.

Give an olive oil spray on the mixture.

Cook for five minutes at 390F.

Open the air fryer and give a toss to the mixture.

cook for five more minutes at 390F.

Take out from air fryer and serve hot.

Nutrition: 350kcal, Protein 22g, Carbs 20g, Fat 6g

Chicken Cheese Quesadilla in Air Fryer

Prep Time: 4 mins

Cook Time: 7 mins

Servings: 4

Ingredients:

- Precooked chicken: one cup, diced
- Tortillas: 2 pieces
- Low-fat cheese: one cup (shredded)

Instructions:

Spray oil the air basket and place one tortilla in it. Add cooked chicken and cheese on top.

Add the second tortilla on top. Put a metal rack on top.

Cook for 6 minutes at 370F, flip it halfway through so cooking evenly.

Slice and serve with dipping sauce.

Nutrition: 171kcal, Protein 15g, Carbs 8g, Fat 8g

Delicious Chicken Pie

Prep Time: 10 mins

Cook Time: 30 mins

Servings: 2

Ingredients:

- *Puff pastry: 2 sheets*

- *Chicken thighs: 2 pieces, cut into cubes*
- *One small onion, chopped*
- *Small potatoes: 2, chopped*
- *Mushrooms: 1/4 cup*
- *Light soya sauce*
- *One carrot, chopped*
- *Black pepper to taste*
- *Worcestershire sauce: to taste*
- *Salt to taste*
- *Italian mixed dried herbs*
- *Garlic powder: a pinch*
- *Plain flour: 2 tbsp.*
- *Milk, as required*
- *Melted butter*

Instructions:

In a mixing bowl, add light soya sauce and pepper add the chicken cubes, and coat well.

In a pan over medium heat, sauté carrot, potatoes, and onion. Add some water, if required, to cook the vegetables.

Add the chicken cubes and mushrooms and cook them too.

Stir in black pepper, salt, Worcestershire sauce, garlic powder, and dried herbs.

When the chicken is cooked through, add some of the flour and mix well.

Add in the milk and let the vegetables simmer until tender.

Place one piece of puff pastry in the baking tray of the air fryer, poke holes with a fork.

Add on top the cooked chicken filling and eggs and puff pastry on top with holes. Cut the excess pastry off. Glaze with oil spray or melted butter

Air fry at 180 F for six minutes, or until it becomes golden brown.

Serve right away and enjoy.

Nutrition: 224kcal, Protein 20g, Carbs 17g, Fat 18 g

Air Fryer Vegetables & Italian Sausage

Prep Time: 5 mins

Cook Time: 14 mins

Servings: 4

Ingredients:

- One bell pepper
- Italian Sausage: 4 pieces spicy or sweet
- One small onion
- 1/4 cup of mushrooms

Instructions:

Let the air fryer pre-heat to 400 F for three minutes.

Put Italian sausage in a single layer in the air fryer basket and let it cook for six minutes.

Slice the vegetables while the sausages are cooking.

After six minutes, reduce the temperature to 360 F. flip the sausage halfway through. Add the mushrooms, onions, and peppers in the basket around the sausage.

Cook at 360 F for 8 minutes. After a 4-minute mix around the sausage and vegetables.

With an instant-read thermometer, the sausage temperature should be 160 F.

Cook more for few minutes if the temperature is not 160F.

Take vegetables and sausage out and serve hot with brown rice.

Nutrition: 291kcal, Protein 16g, Carbs 10g, Fat 21g

Chicken Bites in Air Fryer

Prep Time: 10 mins

Servings: 3

Ingredients:

- *Chicken breast: 2 cups*
- *Kosher salt& pepper to taste*
- *Smashed potatoes: one cup*
- *Scallions: ¼ cup*
- *One Egg beat*
- *Whole wheat breadcrumbs: 1 cup*

Instructions:
Boil the chicken until soft.
Shred the chicken with the help of a fork.
Add the smashed potatoes, scallions to the shredded chicken.
Season with kosher salt and pepper.
Coat with egg and then in bread crumbs.
Put in the air fryer, and cook for 8 minutes at 380F. Or until golden brown.
Serve warm.

Nutrition: 234kcal, Protein 25g, Carbs 15g, Fat 9 g

Popcorn Chicken in Air Fryer

**Prep Time: 10
mins**
                   Cook Time: 20 mins
Servings: 4

Ingredients:
For Marinade:

- *8 cups, chicken tenders, cut into bite-size pieces*
- *Freshly ground black pepper: 1/2 tsp*

- *Almond milk: 2 cups*
- *Salt: 1 tsp*
- *Paprika: 1/2 tsp*

Dry Mix:

- *Salt: 3 tsp*
- *Flour: 3 cups*
- *Paprika: 2 tsp*
- *Oil spray*
- *Freshly ground black pepper: 2 tsp*

Instructions:

In a bowl, add all marinade ingredients and chicken. Mix well, and put it in a ziploc bag and refrigerator for two hours for the minimum, or six hours.

In a large bowl, add all the dry ingredients.

Coat the marinated chicken to the dry mix. Into the marinade again, then for the second time in the dry mixture.

Spray the air fryer basket with olive oil and place the breaded chicken pieces in one single layer. Spray oil over the chicken pieces too.

Cook at 370F for 10 minutes, tossing halfway through.

Serve immediately with salad greens or dipping sauce.

Nutrition: 340kcal, Protein 20g, Carbs 14g, Fat 10g

BEEF RECIPES

Stovetop Meat Loaves

**Prep Time: 30
mins**
             Cook Time: 20 mins

Servings: 2

Ingredients:

- *Three tablespoons 2% milk*
- *Two tablespoons quick-cooking oats*
- *One tablespoon chopped onion*
- *One-eighth tablespoon of salt*
- *Half lb. lean ground beef*
- *¼ tablespoon cornstarch*
- *Half cup Italian tomato sauce*
- *One-fourth cup of cold water*

Instructions

Mix the milk, oats, onion, and salt in a shallow cup. Crumble the beef over the mixture and blend properly. Shape it into 2 loaves. Cook the loaves on all sides in a small nonstick skillet; drain. Mix well the cornstarch, tomato sauce, and water. Pour over beef loaves. Just get it to a boil. Lower the heat to medium-low; cover and simmer for fifteen or twenty minutes, until the meat is no longer pink.

Nutrition: 290 Kcal, Protein 32.1 g, Carbs 11 g, Fat 12.4 g, Sugars 2 g

Spaghetti Pie

Prep Time: 30 mins
       Cook Time: 30 mins
Servings: 6

Ingredients:

- *Six oz uncooked spaghetti*
- *One lb. lean ground beef (90% lean)*
- *Half cup finely chopped onion*
- *One-fourth cup of finely chopped green pepper*

- One cup undrained canned diced tomatoes
- One can (about six oz) tomato paste
- One tablespoon dried oregano
- Three-quarters of tablespoon salt
- Half tablespoon garlic powder
- One-fourth tablespoon of pepper
- ¼ tablespoon of sugar
- Two large egg whites, lightly beaten
- One tablespoon of melted butter
- One-fourth cup of grated Parmesan cheese
- One cup (about eight oz) 2% cottage cheese
- Half cup shredded partly skimmed mozzarella cheese

Instructions

Set the temperature of the oven to 350 ° F. Heat the spaghetti according to the box directions. Then drain.

Cook beef, onion, and green pepper in a large skillet over medium heat for 5-7 minutes or until the beef is no longer pink, slicing the beef into crumbles; drain. Stir in the onions, tomato paste, sugar, and seasonings.

Stir the egg whites, melted butter, and Parmesan cheese in a wide bowl until mixed. To cover, add spaghetti and toss. Press the spaghetti blend on the bottom and sides of a 9-inch greased plate. With crust-forming, deep-dish pie plate. Spread the cottage cheese on the bottom; cover with beef mixture.

Bake for 20 minutes, uncovered. Use the mozzarella cheese for topping. Bake until the cheese is melted and heated properly for an additional 5-10 minutes. Let it stay. Serve after 5 minutes.

Nutrition: 418 Kcal, Protein 36 g, Carbs 29 g, Fat 15.6 g, Sugars 5 g

Beef Stroganoff

Prep Time: 15 mins

Cook Time: 30 mins

Servings: 5

Ingredients:

- *Uncooked Healthy Harvest Whole Grain egg noodles (5 oz)*
- *Olive oil two tablespoons*
- *1 lb. boneless beef tenderloin tips each cut into two inches strips*
- *Half cup onion (minced)*
- *One tablespoon all-purpose flour*
- *Half cup dry white wine*
- *Dijon mustard*
- *one tablespoon beef broth (14.5 ounces fat-free, low-sodium)*

- *Half cup sour cream (fat-free)*
- *¼ tablespoon of salt (optional)*
- *¼ tablespoon of black pepper*
- *One and a half cup sliced white mushrooms*

Instructions

Heat noodles according to package instructions, without adding salt. Add oil over high heat to a large sauté pan. Add meat and sauté for about three minutes. Let the meat out of the pan. Add the onion and mushrooms and sauté for 5 minutes or until brown. Add flour and cook for 1 minute.

In a pan, add wine; cook for 2 minutes. Insert the mustard and beef broth; bring to a boil. Lower the flame and boil for five minutes.

To the broth, add beef and any juices and simmer for 3 more minutes. Add sour cream, pepper, and salt (optional); boil for 30 seconds.

Serve the whole-grain pasta with eggs.

Nutrition: 274 Kcal, Protein 22.1 g, Carbs 28.7 g, Fat 6.8 g, Sugars 2.9 g

Beef with Noodles

Prep Time: 10 mins

   Cook Time: 10 mins

Servings: 4

Ingredients:

- *Three oz package ramen noodles, seasoning packet discarded*
- *One lb. of 90% lean ground beef*
- *One green bell pepper, chopped*

Instructions

- *Half cup onion, chopped*
- *One can (14.5-ounces) diced tomatoes with roasted garlic*
- *One tablespoon Italian seasoning*

- *One tablespoon garlic powder*
- *¼ tablespoon of salt*
- *¼ tablespoon of black pepper*

Cook noodles according to the instructions of the package; rinse and drain.

Add ground beef in a medium nonstick skillet over medium-high heat. Remove and drain the beef.

In the same skillet, cook bell pepper and onions for 5 to 6 minutes, stirring every now and then, over medium heat. Mix the onions, the beef, the Italian seasoning, the garlic, salt, and pepper. Cook for 5 to 7 minutes, or until hot, stirring regularly.

Stir in the noodles and boil for 1 to 2 minutes. And serve.

Nutrition: 324 Kcal, Protein 26 g, Carbs 21.8 g, Fat 13.4 g, Sugars 4.7 g

Cheesy Beef Taco Skillet

Prep Time: 10 mins

Cook Time: 30 mins

Servings: 6

Ingredients:

- *One lb. ground beef*
- *Two cups of cauliflower rice*
- *Ten oz diced tomatoes with green chilies canned*
- *One tablespoon chili powder*
- *One tablespoon cumin ground*
- *One tablespoon salt*
- *Half tablespoon ground black pepper*
- *Half tablespoon onion powder*
- *Eight oz fresh shredded cheese*
- *3.8 oz sliced canned black olives*
- *One shredded lettuce, optional*

Instructions

Heat ground beef in a skillet. Drain.

Make cauliflower rice, if required. (Leftover is perfect in this case). Mix and cook until it starts to boil.

Put chili powder, diced tomatoes, cumin, salt, pepper, onion powder and ground beef.

Reduce temperature. Let it simmer and cook for an additional seven to ten minutes.

Put black olives and one cup of the shredded cheese. Stir it until cheese melts. Top it with the remaining cheese.

Put skillet on the oven broiler at 350 ° F. Wait till the top cheese is totally melted. Serve instantly.

Nutrition: 362 Kcal, Protein 24 g, Carbs 7.7 g, Fat 25.4 g, Sugars 2.9 g

Beef and Ale Casserole

Prep Time: 10 mins

Cook Time: 1 hour

Servings: 4

Ingredients:

- *Three tablespoons plain flour*
- *1 ½ lbs. of leg of beef or diced braising steak*
- *Three tablespoons of olive oil*
- *Two medium onions, cut into big wedges*
- *13 oz of carrots, cut into big chunks*
- *7 oz parsnip, cut into large chunks*

- *2 cups of strong ale*
- *Three tablespoons fresh thyme*
- *One bay leaf*

Instructions

Heat the oven to 340 ° F.

Spread the flour on a dinner plate.

Add beef in the flour.

Pour two tsp of oil into a big frying pan. Fry beef on medium heat for 2-3 minutes. Fry until each side is brown all over.

Shift the meat onto a plate and set aside.

Continue following the above instructions with the remaining meat. You can add more oil if required.

Put the remaining oil in a frying pan. Heat it moderately and sauté the onions, carrots, and parsnips for five minutes.

Then put the beef and vegetables into an ovenproof casserole dish.

Pour in the ale, sprinkle the thyme and bay leaf. Cover with a lid.

Cook in the oven for an hour. Wait till it is properly cooked.

Serve immediately.

Nutrition: 604 Kcal, Protein 59 g, Carbs 33.4 g, Fat 22.7 g

Beef and Veggie Chili

Prep Time: 10 mins

Cook Time: 40 mins

Servings: 6

Ingredients:

- *One tablespoon olive oil*
- *Half lean ground beef*
- *One chopped small onion*
- *One minced clove garlic*
- *One chopped carrot*
- *Two chopped stalks celery*
- *One small chopped bell pepper*
- *Half tablespoon of salt*
- *Half tablespoon cumin*
- *Half tablespoon chili powder*
- *One-quarter tablespoon of cinnamon*
- *Fifteen oz. canned beans, rinsed*
- *Two-third cup of lower-sodium chicken broth*
- *Fourteen and a half ounces of canned diced tomatoes with liquid*
- *salt and pepper*
- *sour cream, if desired*
- *grated cheese*

Instructions

In a medium-sized soup pot, heat oil and then add beef, onion, garlic, carrot, celery, and bell pepper. Continue cooking until the beef is browned, over medium heat. Add all remaining ingredients and stir. Customize seasonings as desired.

Simmer for about 30 minutes over low heat.

Offer with sour cream and grated cheese if desired.

Nutrition: 111 Kcal, Protein 11.4 g, Carbs 19.7 g, Fat 5.7 g, Sugars 5 g

Beef and Red Wine Casserole

Prep Time: 20 mins
Cook Time: 2 hours
Servings: 6

Ingredients:

- 14 oz. of blade steak cubed (extra fat removed)
- One-third cup whole meal plain flour
- One tablespoon olive oil
- One cup red wine
- One-fourth cup of reduced salt beef stock
- 5 cups onions cut into rough wedges
- Two roughly chopped garlic cloves,
- 14 oz. chopped carrots
- Two finely chopped medium celery stalks
- 8 oz. tailed and roughly chopped green beans
- 8 oz. button mushrooms
- 10 oz. unsalted red kidney beans
- 5 cups potatoes washed and roughly chopped into quarters

Instructions

Add steak and flour in a mixing bowl. Toss and coat the steak with the flour.

Add olive oil in a frying pan, heat it moderately, and brown the meat. Remove the meat and set aside. Add the red wine to the pan. Then boil it.

Put the beef stock, onions, garlic, carrots, celery, green beans, mushrooms, kidney beans, and potatoes in the pan.

Let's simmer for five minutes. Let the vegetables soften.

Transfer the meat to the pan. Insert the mixture into a roasting pan.

Put in a heated oven at 350°F for about 2 hours.

Nutrition: 304 Kcal, Protein 16.9 g, Carbs 5.7 g, Fat 1.2 g

Pepper Steak Stew

Prep Time: 5 mins

Cook Time: 2 hours

Servings: 6

Ingredients:

- *1 lb. lean sirloin steak, slice into pieces*
- *Two coarsely chopped green peppers*
- *One diced medium onion*
- *Three large peeled and diced potatoes*
- *3/4 cup of fat-free beef gravy*
- *A quarter tablespoon of dried minced garlic*

Instructions

Spray an ovenproof dish with oil for cooking.

Add steak, green peppers, onion, and potatoes and stir. Add gravy and garlic together.

Bake for about two hours in a 320 ° F oven.

Nutrition: 250 Kcal, Protein 27.4 g, Carbs 15.9 g, Fat 8.5 g

Beef Goulash

Prep Time: 15 mins

Cook Time: 1 hour

Servings: 6

Ingredients:

- *Four tablespoons of olive oil*
- *1,5 lbs. of stewing steak. Sliced into chunks*
- *3 tablespoons of plain flour*
- *One large onion, thinly sliced*
- *Two garlic cloves, finely chopped*
- *One deseeded and thinly sliced green pepper*
- *One deseeded and thinly sliced red pepper*
- *Two tablespoons tomato purée*
- *Two tablespoons paprika*
- *Two large tomatoes, diced*
- *1/3 cup dry white wine*
- *1 cup beef stock, homemade or shop-bought*
- *Two tablespoons parsley leaves*
- *1/2 cup soured cream*

Instructions

Heat oven to 280 ° F.

In a saucepan, heat one tablespoon olive oil. Sprinkle stewed steak chunks with flour and brown well, adding an extra tablespoon of oil. Place aside the browned beef.

Apply to the casserole dish the remaining one tablespoon of oil, followed by onion, garlic cloves, one green pepper, and one finely sliced red pepper. Fry for about 5-10 minutes.

Return the beef with tomato purée and paprika back to the pan. Cook for 2 to 3 minutes, stirring. Add tomatoes, wine, and beef stock. Cover and cook it for about an hour on low heat. Remove the lid after 45 minutes.

Sprinkle parsley leaves with salt and freshly ground pepper and season well. Stir in and add soured cream.

Nutrition: 370 Kcal, Protein 35.1 g, Carbs 31.4 g, Fat 9 g, Sugars 7.1 g

Beef Stew for Diabetics

Prep Time: 20 mins
  Cook Time: 1 hour 30 mins
Servings: 6

Ingredients:

- *Two medium onions*
- *One small peeled celery root*
- *One tablespoon olive oil*
- *One-pound lean stewing beef*
- *Two cloves of garlic*
- *Three cups fat-free broth*
- *A quarter cup barley*
- *Two to three bay leaves*
- *Two cups peeled diced yellow turnips*
- *One medium peeled and diced carrot*
- *One medium peeled and diced potato*
- *One cup cleaned button mushroom*
- *Nineteen oz can stewed tomatoes*
- *One tablespoon savory salt*
- *One tablespoon paprika*
- *Half tablespoon oregano*
- *Half tablespoon cracked black pepper*
- *One tablespoon Worcestershire sauce*

Instructions

Peel and coarsely cut the onions. Coarsely chop the celery as well. Peel the garlic and mince. Sauté until softened in the oil; stir them into a broad stew pot.

In a frying pan, place the beef and cook until browned; whisk in the garlic; then add the onions and celery to the meat. Transfer the water, the barley, and the bay leaves to the stew pot.

Peel and cut into bite-sized bits of all the remaining vegetables. In the order specified, add them to the stew. Then add the spices. Simmer the stew until the meat will be tender.

Add a little more broth as required.

Nutrition: 431 Kcal, Protein 29.4 g, Carbs 32.3 g, Fat 16 g, Sugars 11.1 g

Beef, Artichoke & Mushroom Stew

Prep Time: 20 minutes　　　　　　　　**Cook Time: 2¼ hours**
Servings: 6

Ingredients:

For Beef Marinade:

- *1 onion, chopped*
- *1 garlic clove, crushed*
- *2 tablespoons fresh thyme, hopped*
- *½ cup dry red wine*
- *2 tablespoons tomato puree*
- *2 tablespoons olive oil*
- *1 teaspoon cayenne pepper*
- *Pinch of salt and ground black pepper*
- *1½ pounds beef stew meat, cut into large chunks*

For Stew:

- *2 tablespoons olive oil*
- *2 tablespoons all-purpose flour*
- *½ cup water*
- *½ cup dry red wine*
- *12 ounces jar artichoke hearts, drained and cut into small chunks*
- *4 ounces button mushrooms, sliced*
- *Salt and ground black pepper, as required*

Instructions:

For marinade: in a large bowl, add all the ingredients except the beef and mix well.

Add the beef and coat with the marinade generously. Refrigerate to marinate overnight.

Remove the beef from bowl, reserving the marinade.
In a large pan, heat the oil and sear the beef in 2 batches for about 5 minutes or until browned.
With a slotted spoon, transfer the beef into a bowl.
In the same pan, add the reserved marinade, flour, water and wine and stir to combine.
Stir in the cooked beef and bring to a boil.
Reduce the heat to low and simmer, covered for about 2 hours, stirring occasionally.
Stir in the artichoke hearts and mushrooms and simmer for about 30 minutes.
Stir in the salt and black pepper and bring to a boil over high heat.
Remove from the eat ad serve hot.

Nutrition: Calories 367, Fat 16.6 g, Carbs 9.6 g, Sugar 2.2 g, Protein 36.7 g

AIR FRY RECIPES

Air Fried Beef Schnitzel

Prep Time: 10 mins

Cook Time: 15 mins

Servings: 1

Ingredients:

- *One lean beef schnitzel*
- *Olive oil: 2 tablespoon*
- *Breadcrumbs: ¼ cup*
- *One egg*
- *One lemon, to serve*

Instructions:

Let the air fryer heat to 356F.

In a big bowl, add breadcrumbs and oil, mix well until forms a crumbly mixture

Dip beef steak in whisked egg and coat in breadcrumbs mixture.

Place the breaded beef in the air fryer and cook at 356F for 15 minutes or more until fully cooked through.

Take out from the air fryer and serve with the side of salad greens and lemon.

Nutrition: 340kcal, Proteins 20g, Carbs 14g, Fat 10g

Air Fryer Meatloaf

**Prep Time: 10
mins**
       Cook Time: 40 mins
Servings: 8

Ingredients:

- *Ground lean beef: 4 cups*
- *Bread crumbs: 1 cup (soft and fresh)*
- *Chopped mushrooms: ½ cup*
- *Cloves of minced garlic*
- *Shredded carrots: ½ cup*
- *Beef broth: ¼ cup*
- *Chopped onions: ½ cup*
- *Two eggs beaten*
- *Ketchup: 3 Tbsp.*
- *Worcestershire sauce: 1 Tbsp.*
- *Dijon mustard: 1 Tbsp.*

For Glaze:

- *Ketchup: half cup*
- *Dijon mustard: 2 tsp*

Instructions:
In a big bowl, add beef broth and breadcrumbs, stir well. And set it aside in a food processor, add garlic, onions, mushrooms, and carrots, and pulse on high until finely chopped.
In a separate bowl, add soaked breadcrumbs, Dijon mustard, Worcestershire sauce, eggs, lean ground beef, ketchup, and salt. With your hands, combine well and make it into a loaf.
Let the air fryer preheat to 390 F.
Put Meatloaf in the Air Fryer and let it cook for 45 minutes.
In the meantime, add Dijon mustard, ketchup, and brown sugar in a bowl and mix. Glaze this mix over Meatloaf when five minutes are left.

Rest the Meatloaf for ten minutes before serving.

Nutrition: 330 kcal, Proteins 19g, Carbs 16g, Fat 9.9 g

Air Fried Steak with Asparagus Bundles

Prep Time: 20 mins
   Cook Time: 30 mins
Servings: 2

Ingredients:

- Olive oil spray
- Flank steak (2 pounds)- cut into 6 pieces
- Kosher salt and black pepper
- Two cloves of minced garlic
- Asparagus: 4 cups
- Tamari sauce: half cup
- Three bell peppers: sliced thinly
- Beef broth: 1/3 cup
- 1 Tbsp. of unsalted butter
- Balsamic vinegar: 1/4 cup

Instructions:
Sprinkle salt and pepper on steak and rub.
In a ziploc bag, add garlic and Tamari sauce, then add steak, toss well and seal the bag.
Let it marinate for one hour to overnight.
Equally, place bell peppers and asparagus in the center of the steak. Roll the steak around the vegetables and secure well with toothpicks.
Preheat the air fryer.
Spray the steak with olive oil spray. And place steaks in the air fryer.
Cook for 15 minutes at 400F or more till steaks are cooked
Take the steak out from the air fryer and let it rest for five minute

Remove steak bundles and allow them to rest for 5 minutes before serving/slicing.

In the meantime, add butter, balsamic vinegar, and broth over medium flame. Mix well and reduce it by half. Add salt and pepper to taste.

Pour over steaks right before serving.

Nutrition: 471kcal, Protein 29g, Carbs 20g, Fat 15g

Air Fryer Hamburgers

Prep Time: 5 mins

  Cook Time: 13 mins

Servings: 4

Ingredients:

- *Buns:4*
- *Lean ground beef chuck: 4 cups*
- *Salt to taste*
- *Slices of any cheese: 4 slices*
- *Black Pepper, to taste*

Instructions:
Let the air fryer preheat to 350 F.

In a bowl, add lean ground beef, pepper, and salt. Mix well and form patties.

Put them in the air fryer in one layer only, cook for 6 minutes, flip them halfway through. One minute before you take out the patties, add cheese on top.

When cheese is melted, take out from the air fryer.

Add ketchup, any dressing to your buns, add tomatoes and lettuce and patties.

Serve hot.

Nutrition: 520kcal, Protein 31g, Carbs 22g, Fat 34g

Air Fryer Beef Steak Kabobs with Vegetables

Prep Time: 5 mins

Cook Time: 13 mins

Servings: 4

Ingredients:

- *Light Soy sauce: 2 tbsp.*
- *Lean beef chuck ribs: 4 cups, cut into one-inch pieces*
- *Low-fat sour cream: 1/3 cup*
- *Half onion*
- *8 skewers: 6 inch*
- *One bell peppers*

Instructions:

In a mixing bowl, add soy sauce and sour cream, mix well. Add the lean beef chunks, coat well, and let it marinate for half an hour or more.

Cut onion, bell pepper into one-inch pieces. In water, soak skewers for ten minutes.

Add onions, bell peppers, and beef on skewers; alternatively, sprinkle with Black Pepper

Let it cook for 10 minutes in a preheated air fryer at 400F, flip halfway through.

Serve with yogurt dipping sauce.

Nutrition: 268kcal, Protein 20g, Carbs 15g, Fat 10g

Air Fried Empanadas

Prep Time: 10 mins

   Cook Time: 20 mins

Servings: 2

Ingredients:

- *Square gyoza wrappers: eight pieces*
- *Olive oil: 1 tablespoon*
- *White onion: 1/4 cup, finely diced*
- *Mushrooms: 1/4 cup, finely diced*
- *Half cup lean ground beef*
- *Chopped garlic: 2 teaspoons*
- *Paprika: 1/4 teaspoon*
- *Ground cumin: 1/4 teaspoon*
- *Six green olives, diced*
- *Ground cinnamon: 1/8 teaspoon*
- *Diced tomatoes: half cup*
- *One egg, lightly beaten*

Instructions:

In a skillet, over a medium flame, add oil, onions, and beef and cook for 3 minutes, until beef turns brown.

Add mushrooms and cook for six minutes until it starts to brown. Then add paprika, cinnamon, olives, cumin, and garlic and cook for 3 minutes or more.

Add in the chopped tomatoes, and cook for a minute. Turn off the heat; let it cool for five minutes.

Lay gyoza wrappers on a flat surface add one and a half tbsp. of beef filling in each wrapper. Brush edges with water or egg, fold wrappers, pinch edges.

Put four empanadas in an even layer in an air fryer basket, and cook for 7 minutes at 400°F until nicely browned.

Serve with sauce and salad greens.

Nutrition: 343kcal, Protein 18g, Carbohydrate 12.9g, Fat 19g

Air Fry Rib-Eye Steak

Prep Time: 5 mins
Cook Time: 14 mins
Servings: 2

Ingredients:

*   *Lean rib eye steaks: 2 medium-sized*
*   *Salt & freshly ground black pepper, to taste*

Instructions:
Let the air fry preheat at 400 F. pat dry steaks with paper towels.
Use any spice blend or just salt and pepper on steaks.
Generously on both sides of the steak.
Put steaks in the air fryer basket. Cook according to the rareness you want. Or cook for 14 minutes and flip after half time.
Take out from the air fryer and let it rest for about 5 minutes.
Serve with microgreen salad.

Nutrition: 470kcal, Protein 45g, Carbs 23g, Fat 31g

PORK RECIPES

Braised Pork with Mushrooms and Butter Beans

Prep Time: 15 mins

Cook Time: 1 hour 15 mins

Servings: 6

Ingredients:

- *1 lb. cubed lean pork*
- *One thinly sliced large onion*
- *Two crushed cloves of garlic*
- *One thinly sliced leek*
- *1 tablespoon of plain flour*

- *1,5 cups of sliced mushrooms*
- *Two tablespoons of Dijon mustard*
- *One vegetable stock cube, dissolved in 1,5 cups water*
- *15 oz. of drained tin butter beans*

Instructions

In a saucepan, warm the oil and add the cubed pork. Stir-fry until browned for 3-4 minutes. Then add the onions, garlic, and leek. Stir and fry for an extra 3-4 minutes before tender. Sprinkle and blend with the flour. Insert the mushrooms, mustard, and stock, stirring continually to get to a gentle boil.

Move the heat down to medium, cover the lid and gently boil for 1 hour, stirring regularly and, if possible, adding a little more water.

Add the butter beans, stir, and boil for an additional ten minutes before serving.

Nutrition: 184 Kcal, Protein 22.3 g, Carbs 10 g, Fat 5 g, Sugars 3.1 g

Pulled Pork

Prep Time: 15 mins

Cook Time: 50 mins

Servings: 4

Ingredients:

- *One tablespoon paprika*
- *One tablespoon chili powder*
- *A quarter tablespoon salt*
- *One eighth tablespoon Cayenne pepper*
- *One-pound pork tenderloin, trimmed of all visible fat*
- *Three tablespoons of olive oil*
- *One small onion, diced*
- *One garlic clove, minced*

- *One (8 oz) can no-salt-added tomato sauce*
- *Two tablespoons apple cider vinegar*
- *Two cups thinly sliced cabbage*
- *One medium carrot, peeled and coarsely shredded*
- *One small red apple, cored and cut into thin strips*
- *Two tablespoons apple cider vinegar*
- *One-eighth tablespoon of celery seeds*

Instructions

Stir together the paprika, chili powder, spice, and pepper in a small bowl to dress the pork.

Break the pork into 2-inch strips. Sprinkle half of the mixture of paprika all over the pork.

Heat two teaspoons of olive oil over medium heat in a wide skillet. Add the pork and cook until browned on all sides, turning occasionally, for about 6 minutes. To a plate, transfer the pork.

Put the remaining 1 teaspoon of olive oil in the skillet. Add the onion and cook for around 3 minutes, stirring sometimes, before it starts to soften. Apply the garlic and the remaining paprika mixture and simmer for around 30 seconds, stirring continuously, until fragrant.

Add the tomato sauce, vinegar, and stir to mix well. Add the pork and any leftover juices, reduce the heat to very minimal, cover, and cook until the pork is tender, stirring periodically, for around 25 minutes.

Withdraw the skillet from the heat. Shred the pork in the skillet into pieces using 2 forks.

Nutrition: 250 Kcal, Protein 25.3 g, Carbs 18 g, Fat 8.1 g, Sugars 12 g

Herb-Crusted Pork Chops

Prep Time: 5 mins

Cook Time: 10 mins

Servings: 6

Ingredients:

- *One tablespoon dried rosemary*
- *One tablespoon dried oregano*
- *Half tablespoon dried thyme*
- *Half tablespoon garlic powder*
- *Half tablespoon chili powder*
- *A quarter tablespoon black pepper*

- *One tablespoon olive oil*
- *1 lb. of boneless chops pork loin*

Instructions

Combine the rosemary, oregano, thyme, garlic, chili, and black pepper in a shallow cup. Mix thoroughly.

In a large saucepan, add olive oil and heat over medium-high heat. Season the pork chops with herb mixture.

Sauté chops of pork for approximately 5 minutes per side or until cooked.

Nutrition: 162 Kcal, Protein 23 g, Carbs 0.9 g, Fat 6.1 g, Sugars 0 g

25-Minute Pork Loin

Prep Time: 10 mins

Cook Time: 15 mins

Servings: 4

Ingredients:

- *One tablespoon water*
- *One tablespoon Worcestershire sauce*
- *One tablespoon lemon juice*

- One tablespoon Dijon-style mustard
- Four boneless pork top loin chops
- Half tablespoon lemon-pepper seasoning
- One tablespoon butter
- One tablespoon snipped fresh chives

Instructions

For the sauce, combine water, Worcestershire sauce, lemon juice, and mustard in a small bowl; set aside.

Trim fat from chops. Use the lemon-pepper seasoning to sprinkle both sides of each chop. In a 10-inch pan, melt butter over medium heat. Add chops and cook for 8 to 12 minutes. Rotating once halfway through the cooking period. Withdraw from the heat.

Place chops to a serving platter; protect and hold warm.

Pour the sauce into the pan; stir and extract any crusty brown pieces from the bottom of the pan. Pour the gravy over the chops. Sprinkle chives.

Nutrition: 176 Kcal, Protein 18.2 g, Carbs 1 g, Fat 10.4 g

Pork Chop Casserole

Prep Time: 10 mins

Cook Time: 40 mins

Servings: 4

Ingredients:

- One tablespoon canola oil
- One onion, cut into quarter-inch thick strips
- A quarter cup all-purpose flour
- A quarter tsp salt
- Half tablespoon black pepper
- Four pork loin chops (about Half-inch thick)
- One can reduced-sodium condensed cream of mushroom soup

- *Two tablespoons Dijon-style mustard*
- *Three fourth cup low-sodium chicken broth*
- *Half tablespoon dried thyme leaves*
- *One cup sliced mushrooms*

Instructions

Preheat the oven to 350 ° F. Using cooking spray to powder a 9 x 13-inch baking dish.

Heat the oil and sauté the onions for 10 to 12 minutes or until golden in a wide skillet over medium-high heat. Withdraw to a tray.

Combine the flour, salt, and pepper in a shallow dish; blend well.

Coat the pork chops evenly on both sides in a flour mixture.

Cook the pork chops in the same skillet with onion for 4-5 minutes over medium-high heat or until browned on both sides.

Add the remaining ingredients in a medium saucepan. Pour the chops and bake in the oven for 25 to 30 minutes.

Nutrition: 250 Kcal, Protein 21 g, Carbs 15 g, Fat 10.7 g, Sugars 3.1 g

Baked Boneless Pork Chops in Tomato Sauce

Prep Time: 5 mins

Cook Time: 25 mins

Servings: 4

Ingredients:

- *Four pork chops*
- *One yellow onion*
- *Four cloves of garlic*
- *1,5 lbs. diced canned tomatoes*
- *Five ounces low-fat mozzarella*
- *One chicken bouillon cube*
- *One tablespoon paprika*

- *One tablespoon dried oregano*
- *Salt and pepper to taste*
- *Cooking spray*

Instructions

Preheat a 400 F oven.

Split the onions into rings. Peel the garlic and break it.

Coat a pan with cooking spray and place over medium-high heat.
Season the pork chops with pepper and sear on each side for
approximately 2 minutes (until light brown).

Remove the pork chops from the heat and place them in a deep pan
for baking. Add the onion rings and garlic, the bouillon cube, and
spices and blend them all together. Let it boil for 2 minutes.

Pour the tomato sauce and add mozzarella on top.

Put it all in a baking dish and after in the oven. Baking for 20
minutes.

Take the pork chops out of the oven and allow them to rest before
serving for 5 minutes in the pan.

Nutrition: 401 Kcal, Protein 42.3 g, Carbs 16 g, Fat 17 g, Sugars
6.2 g

Jamaican Pork Tenderloin

**Prep Time: 10
mins**
        Cook Time: 25 mins
Servings: 4

Ingredients:

- *One tablespoon ground allspice*
- *One tablespoon ground cinnamon*
- *Half tablespoon ground ginger*
- *Half tablespoon onion powder*

- *Half tablespoon garlic powder*
- *A quarter tablespoon Cayenne pepper*
- *two ground cloves*
- *Three quarters tablespoon salt*
- *Half tablespoon ground black pepper freshly ground*
- *One pork tenderloin about 1 lb. trimmed of visible fat*
- *Two tablespoons white vinegar*
- *One tablespoon tomato paste*

Instructions

Mix the allspice, cinnamon, ginger, onion powder, garlic powder, cayenne, cloves, half a tsp of salt, and black pepper in a small bowl. Rub the mixture of spices over the pork and let it stand for 15 minutes.

Mix the tomato paste and the remaining quarter of a tablespoon of salt in another little cup.

On the grill rack or broiler plate, put the pork. At medium-high heat, grill or broil, turning several times, until browned on all sides, for a total of 3 to 4 minutes. Remove from the grill and put to a cooler section (or reduce the fire) and proceed to cook for 14 minutes. Baste with vinegar and proceed to cook until an instant-read thermometer inserted into the thickest section reads 160 F. Switch to a cutting board, and allow cool for 5 minutes before slicing.

Nutrition: 170 Kcal, Protein 27 g, Carbs 6.3 g, Fat 6.1 g, Sugars 4 g

Pork Ribs

Prep Time: 5 mins
Cook Time: 30 mins
Servings: 4

Ingredients:

- *Sixteen pork ribs*

- *Half cup hoisin sauce*

- *Two and a half tablespoon soy sauce*
- *One and a half tablespoon red wine vinegar*
- *Two tablespoons Chinese spice powder*

Instructions

Preheat the oven at 360 ° F.

Cook the ribs in a large saucepan, coated with water. Carry the water to a boil and cook for twenty minutes.

Mix the hoisin sauce, soy sauce, wine vinegar, and spice powder in a small bowl.

Brush this glaze all over the ribs after draining the ribs.

Place and cook on a baking tray for 30 minutes.

Nutrition: 321 Kcal, Protein 21.7 g, Carbs 4.9 g, Fat 24.3 g, Sugars 2.6 g

Pork Tenderloin Fajitas

Prep Time: 5 mins
Cook Time: 25 mins
Servings: 15

Ingredients:

- *Four pork tenderloins (3-4 lbs.)*
- *Half cup fajita marinade*

Instructions

Place the tenderloins in a wide self-sealing bag; pour over the marinade. Refrigerate and seal the bag for 24 hours.

Heat oven to 450 degrees F. Remove the tenderloins (discard the remaining marinade) from the bag, and place them in a shallow roasting pan. Roasted the tenderloins for 20-25 minutes until the internal temperature (measured by a meat thermometer) is 160 degrees F. Remove from the oven, cut into slices to serve.

Nutrition: 130 Kcal, Protein 23.6 g, Carbs 1 g, Fat 3.2 g

Pork Loin Roulades

Prep Time: 10 mins
Cook Time: 45 mins
Servings: 4

Ingredients:

- 2 lbs. of sliced pork loin
- 2 garlic cloves
- 8 sage leaves
- ½ cup of dry white wine
- ¼ cup of olive oil
- Salt and pepper to taste

Instructions
Flatten the pork slices, place a clove of garlic and a sage leaf on top, roll up and secure using a toothpick.
Heat the oil in a frying pan, place the roulades and brown over high heat on both sides, for even and homogeneous cooking. Lower the heat, add a little wine and water, salt and pepper to taste and leave to cook for about 30 minutes, until the meat is tender.

Nutrition: Calories 165.3 kcal, Carbs 1.3 g, Protein 22.3 g, Fat 9.4 g

Pork Stew

Prep Time: 30 mins
Cook Time: 1 hour 50 mins
Servings: 6

Ingredients:

- *1 lb. and 8 oz of pork meat in pieces*
- *6 sausages*
- *2 garlic cloves*
- *1 onion*
- *3 cups of tomato paste*
- *½ glass of red wine*
- *1 bay leaf*
- *Salt and pepper*

Instructions
Prick the sausages with a fork and blanch in a little water with the peeled garlic, to be removed at the end of cooking, and oil. Add the bay leaf and the pork meat, brown everything over a low heat, turning from time to time with a wooden spoon to even out the cooking. Deglaze with the wine. Adjust the salt and cook for 40 minutes over medium heat. Then add sausages and finish cooking for one hour.

Nutrition: Calories 248.6 kcal, Carbs 7.1 g, Protein 6.2 g, Fat 2.8 g

AIR FRY RECIPES

Air Fryer Breaded Pork Chops

Prep Time: 10 mins

Cook Time: 12 mins

Servings: 4

Ingredients:

- *Whole-wheat breadcrumbs: 1 cup*
- *Salt: ¼ teaspoon*
- *Pork chops: 2-4 pieces (center cut and boneless)*

- *Chili powder: half teaspoon*
- *Parmesan cheese: 1 tablespoon*
- *Paprika: 1½ teaspoons*
- *One egg beaten*
- *Onion powder: half teaspoon*
- *Granulated garlic: half teaspoon*
- *Pepper, to taste*

Instructions:

Let the air fryer preheat to 400 F

Rub kosher salt on each side of pork chops, let it rest

Add beaten egg in a big bowl

Add Parmesan cheese, breadcrumbs, garlic, pepper, paprika, chili powder, and onion powder in a bowl and mix well

Dip pork chop in egg, then in breadcrumb mixture

Put it in the air fryer and spray with oil.

Let it cook for 12 minutes at 400 F. flip it over halfway through. Cook for another six minutes.

Serve with a side of salad.

Nutrition: 425 kcal, Protein 31 g, Carbs 19g, Fat 20g, Fiber 5g

Pork Taquitos in Air Fryer

**Prep Time: 10
mins**
        Cook Time: 20 mins
Servings: 10

Ingredients:

- *Pork tenderloin: 3 cups, cooked & shredded*
- *Cooking spray*
- *Shredded mozzarella: 2 and 1/2 cups, fat-free*
- *10 small tortillas*
- *Salsa for dipping*
- *One juice of a lime*

Instructions:
Let the air fryer preheat to 380 F
Add lime juice to pork and mix well
With a damp towel over the tortilla, microwave for ten seconds to soften
Add pork filling and cheese on top, in a tortilla, roll up the tortilla tightly.
Place tortillas on a greased foil pan
Spray oil over tortillas. Cook for 7-10 minutes or until tortillas is golden brown, flip halfway through.
Serve with fresh salad.

Nutrition: 253kcal, Protein 20g, Carbs 10g, Fat 18g

Air Fryer Tasty Egg Rolls

Prep Time: 10 mins

   Cook Time: 20 mins

Servings: 3

Ingredients:

- *Coleslaw mix: half bag*
- *Half onion*
- *Salt: 1/2 teaspoon*
- *Half cups of mushrooms*
- *Lean ground pork: 2 cups*
- *One stalk of celery*
- *Wrappers (egg roll)*

Instructions:

Put a skillet over medium flame, add onion and lean ground pork and cook for 5-7 minutes.

Add coleslaw mixture, salt, mushrooms, and celery to skillet and cook for almost five minutes.

Lay egg roll wrapper flat and add filling (1/3 cup), roll it up, seal with water.

Spray with oil the rolls.

Put in the air fryer for 6-8 minutes at 400F, flipping once halfway through.

Serve hot.

Nutrition: 245kcal, Protein 11g, Carbs 9g, Fat 10g

Pork Dumplings in Air Fryer

Prep Time: 30 mins

   Cook Time: 20 mins

Servings: 6

Ingredients:

- *18 dumpling wrappers*
- *One teaspoon olive oil*

- *Bok choy: 4 cups (chopped)*
- *Rice vinegar: 2 tablespoons*
- *Diced ginger: 1 tablespoon*
- *Crushed red pepper: 1/4 teaspoon*
- *Diced garlic: 1 tablespoon*
- *Lean ground pork: half cup*
- *Cooking spray*
- *Lite soy sauce: 2 teaspoons*
- *Honey: half tsp.*
- *Toasted sesame oil: 1 teaspoon*
- *Finely chopped scallions*

Instructions:

In a large skillet, heat olive oil, add bok choy, cook for 6 minutes, and add garlic, ginger, and cook for one minute. Move this mixture on a paper towel and pat dry the excess oil

In a bowl, add bok choy mixture, crushed red pepper, and lean ground pork and mix well.

Lay a dumpling wrapper on a plate and add one tbsp. of filling in the wrapper's middle. With water, seal the edges and crimp it.

Air spray the air fryer basket, add dumplings in the air fryer basket and cook at 375 F for 12 minutes or until browned.

In the meantime, to make the sauce, add sesame oil, rice vinegar, scallions, soy sauce, and honey in a bowl mix together.

Serve the dumplings with sauce.

Nutrition: 140kcal, Protein 12g, Carbohydrate 9g, Fat 5g

Air Fryer Pork Chop & Broccoli

Prep Time: 20 mins

Cook Time: 20 mins

Servings: 2

Ingredients:

- *Broccoli florets: 2 cups*
- *Bone-in pork chop: 2 pieces*
- *Paprika: half tsp.*
- *Avocado oil: 2 tbsp.*
- *Garlic powder: half tsp.*
- *Onion powder: half tsp.*
- *Two cloves of crushed garlic*
- *Salt: 1 teaspoon divided*

Instructions:

Let the air fryer preheat to 350F. Spray the basket with cooking oil
Add one tbsp. Oil, onion powder, half tsp. of salt, garlic powder, and paprika in a bowl mix well, rub this spice mix to the pork chop's sides
Add pork chops to air fryer basket and let it cook for five minutes
In the meantime, add one tsp. oil, garlic, half tsp of salt, and broccoli to a bowl and coat well
Flip the pork chop and add the broccoli, let it cook for five more minutes.
Take out from the air fryer and serve.

Nutrition: 483kcal, Protein 23g, Carbs 12g, Fat 20g

Cheesy Pork Chops in Air Fryer

Prep Time: 5 mins
       Cook Time: 8 mins
Servings: 2

Ingredients:

- *4 lean pork chops*
- *Salt: half tsp.*

- *Garlic powder: half tsp.*
- *Shredded cheese: 4 tbsp.*
- *Chopped cilantro*

Instructions:
Let the air fryer preheat to 350F.

With garlic, cilantro, and salt, rub the pork chops. Put in the air fryer. Let it cook for four minutes. Flip them and cook for two minutes more.

Add cheese on top of them and cook for another two minutes or until the cheese is melted.

Serve with salad greens.

Nutrition: 467kcal, Protein 61g, Fat 22g

Pork Rind Nachos

Prep Time: 5 mins
       Cook Time: 5 mins
Servings: 2

Ingredients:

- *2 tbsp. of pork rinds*
- *1/4 cup shredded cooked chicken*
- *1/2 cup shredded Monterey jack cheese*
- *1/4 cup sliced pickled jalapeños*
- *1/4 cup guacamole*
- *1/4 cup full-fat sour cream*

Instructions:
Put pork rinds in a 6 "round baking pan. Fill with grilled chicken and Monterey cheese jack. Place the pan in the basket with the air fryer.

Set the temperature to 370 ° F and set the timer for 5 minutes or until the cheese has been melted.
Eat right away with jalapeños, guacamole, and sour cream.

Nutrition: 295kcal, Protein 30.1 g, Carbs 3g, Fat 27.5 g

Jamaican Jerk Pork in Air Fryer

Prep Time: 10 mins
> **Cook Time: 20 mins**
Servings: 4

Ingredients:

- *Pork, cut into three-inch pieces*
- *Jerk paste: ¼ cup*

Instructions:
Rub jerk paste all over the pork pieces.
Let it marinate for four hours, at least, in the refrigerator. Or for more time.
Let the air fryer preheat to 390 F. spray with olive oil
Before putting in the air fryer, let the meat sit for 20 minutes at room temperature.
Cook for 20 minutes at 390 F in the air fryer, flip halfway through.
Take out from the air fryer let it rest for ten minutes before slicing.
Serve with microgreens.

Nutrition: 234kcal, Protein 31g, Carbs 12g, Fat 9g

Pork Tenderloin with Mustard Glazed

Prep Time: 10 mins

Cook Time: 18 mins
Servings: 4

Ingredients:

- *Yellow mustard: ¼ cup*
- *One pork tenderloin*
- *Salt: ¼ tsp*
- *Freshly ground black pepper: ⅛ tsp*
- *Minced garlic: 1 Tbsp.*
- *Dried rosemary: 1 tsp*
- *Italian seasoning: 1 tsp*

Instructions:

With a knife, cut the top of pork tenderloin. Add garlic (minced) in the cuts. Then sprinkle with kosher salt and pepper.

In a bowl, add mustard, rosemary, and Italian seasoning mix until combined. Rub this mustard mix all over pork.

Let it marinate in the refrigerator for at least two hours.

Put pork tenderloin in the air fryer basket. Cook for 18-20 minutes at 400 F. with an instant-read thermometer internal temperature of pork should be 145 F

Take out from the air fryer and serve with a side of salad.

Nutrition: 390kcal, Protein 59g, Carbs 11g, Fat 11g

LAMB RECIPES

Lamb Provenç al

Prep Time: 5 mins

Cook Time: 30 mins

Servings: 4

Ingredients:

- *Two tablespoons rapeseed oil*
- *Two chopped onions*
- *One red pepper (chopped into large chunks)*

- *One yellow pepper (chopped into large chunks)*
- *One green pepper (chopped into large chunks)*
- *Four to six crushed cloves of garlic*
- *Two to three courgettes*
- *One sprig rosemary*
- *One sprig thyme*
- *One tablespoon dried oregano*
- *Fresh parsley*
- *14 oz. chopped tomatoes*
- *4 lean lamb steaks*

Instructions

Add oil to a pan. Add the onions, and over medium heat, stir for 2 minutes. Then introduce the peppers, red, yellow, and green, and mix for another 2 minutes. Apply the courgettes and garlic and stir for 2-3 minutes.

Combine the vegetables with the rosemary, thyme, oregano, and parsley, and then tomatoes. Cover and simmer gently, stirring occasionally for 10 minutes.

Grill the lamb steaks and simmer until well cooked.

Remove the meat from the heat, cover it, and leave for 3 minutes to rest. Serve with sauce from Provence.

Nutrition: 251 Kcal, Protein 26 g, Carbs 13.2 g, Fat 8.1 g, Sugars 10.1 g

Lamb Kebabs with Verdant Salsa

Prep Time: 5 mins

Cook Time: 15 mins

Servings: 4

Ingredients:

Kebab mix

- *14 oz. minced lamb*
- *Two tablespoons garlic, peeled and finely chopped*
- *Two tablespoons ginger, peeled and finely chopped*
- *One large peeled and chopped onion*
- *Three tablespoons ground coriander*
- *Two tablespoons ground cumin*
- *A quarter tablespoon of ground black pepper*

Verdant salsa mix

- *Three chopped spring onions*
- *One tablespoon olive oil*
- *Four tomatoes, chopped roughly*
- *One tablespoon pitted olives of your choice*
- *One bunch of chopped coriander*
- *One bunch of chopped parsley*
- *Juice of a lemon*

Instructions

In a mixing bowl, combine the onion, ginger, garlic, coriander, cumin, pepper, and salt. Add the minced lamb and mix well all the ingredients.

Prepare 16 balls from the mince mixture.

Place each ball around a metal skewer's tip and flatten it slightly.

Put and cover the meatballs on a baking sheet, then refrigerate them for an hour.

Blend all the salsa verdant ingredients in a bowl.

Cook the skewered lamb kebabs under a preheated grill, rotating, until the lamb is cooked through. It will take fifteen minutes.

Serve warm with salsa.

Nutrition: 310 Kcal, Protein 19.7 g, Carbs 10 g, Fat 18.3 g

Herb-Crusted Rack of Lamb

Prep Time: 5 mins (plus marinating time)

Cook Time:

20 mins

Servings: 4

Ingredients:

- *Four minced cloves of garlic*
- *Half cup of chopped fresh rosemary leaves*
- *A quarter cup of chopped fresh mint leaves*

- *Salt to taste*
- *Fresh ground black pepper*
- *One rack of lamb, trimmed*
- *Half cup chopped fresh parsley leaves*

- *One cup bread crumbs*
- *One tablespoon Dijon mustard*

Instructions

Stir together the garlic, salt, pepper, rosemary, and mint in a shallow dish. Rub the mixture over the lamb and refrigerate, overnight.

In a shallow bowl, combine the bread crumbs and parsley. Season with salt and pepper, and set aside.

Using nonstick spray to spray a roasting pan. Put the lamb (meat side down), and cook for 10 minutes to 400 ° F.

Switch up the side of the lamb meat and spray the meat with the mustard. Over the mustard, spread the crumb mixture and press it onto the meat. Return to the oven and cook for 10 more minutes. Enable the meat for 5 minutes to rest before serve.

Nutrition: 321 Kcal, Protein 34.5 g, Carbs 22 g, Fat 11 g

Chutney Lamb Chops

Prep Time: 10 mins

Cook Time: 25 mins

Servings: 4

Ingredients:

- *Four lamb loin chops (5 ounces each)*
- *Half cup of water*
- *A quarter cup dried cranberry*
- *A quarter cup dried apricot, cut into quarters*
- *A quarter cup no-sugar-added raspberry fruit spread*
- *One tablespoon red wine vinegar*
- *A quarter tablespoon ground cinnamon*
- *One-eighth tablespoon of salt*
- *One peeled medium pear (sliced into half-inch pieces)*
- *Half tablespoon vanilla*
- *Two minced cloves of garlic*
- *A quarter tablespoon of crushed dried rosemary*
- *Black pepper*

Instructions

Preheat the broiler.

Combine cranberries, water, apricots, fruit spread, vinegar, cinnamon, and salt in a medium saucepan to produce the chutney. Bring the mixture over high heat to a simmer.

Reduce heat to medium-low and cook uncovered for 12 minutes or until thickened by the mixture. Remove from the heat; introduce the pear and vanilla and stir.

Rub the lamb chops with garlic on all ends. Sprinkle with rosemary, and pepper.

Coat the broiler pan and rack with non-stick cooking spray and arrange the lamb chops.

Broil lamb for 7 minutes, (ensuring they are at least 5 inches from the source of the fire).

Turnover and broil for 7 more minutes or until necessary.

Serve lamb chops with chutney sauce.

Nutrition: 253 Kcal, Protein 21 g, Carbs 23 g, Fat 7 g

Greek Style Mini Burger Pies

Prep Time: 15 minutes   **Cook Time:**
40 minutes
Servings: 6

Ingredients:

Burger mixture:

- *Onion, large, chopped (1 piece)*
- *Red bell peppers, roasted, diced (1/2 cup)*
- *Ground lamb, 80% lean (1 pound)*
- *Red pepper flakes (1/4 teaspoon)*
- *Feta cheese, crumbled (2 ounces)*

Baking mixture:

- *Milk (1/2 cup)*
- *Biscuit mix, classic (1/2 cup)*
- *Eggs (2 pieces)*

Instructions:
Preheat oven at 350 degrees F.
Grease 12 muffin cups using cooking spray.
Cook the onion and meat in a skillet heated on medium-high. Once lamb is browned and cooked through, drain and let cool for five minutes. Stir together with feta cheese, roasted red peppers, and red pepper flakes.
Whisk the baking mixture ingredients together. Fill each muffin cup with baking mixture (1 tablespoon).
Air-fry for twenty-five to thirty minutes. Let cool before serving.

Nutrition: Calories 270; Fat 10 g; Protein 10 g; Carbs 10 g

Leg of Lamb with Potatoes

Prep   **Time:**   **20**
mins
              Cook Time: 1¼ hours
Servings: 8

Ingredients:

- *1 (4-pound) bone in leg of lamb, fat trimmed*
- *Salt and ground black pepper, as required*
- *5 garlic cloves, sliced*
- *8 medium potatoes, peeled and cut into wedges*
- *1 medium onion, peeled and cut into wedges*

- *1 teaspoon garlic powder*
- *1 teaspoon paprika*
- *2 cups water*

For Spice Mixture:

- *½ cup olive oil*
- *¼ cup fresh lemon juice*
- *5 garlic cloves, peeled*
- *2 tablespoons dried mint*
- *2 tablespoons dried oregano*
- *1 tablespoon paprika*
- *½ tablespoon ground nutmeg*

Instructions

Remove the leg of lamb from the refrigerator and set aside in room temperature for about 1 hour before cooking.

For spice mixture: in a food processor, add all the ingredients and pulse until smooth.

Transfer the spice mixture into a bowl and set aside.

Preheat the broiler of the oven.

With paper towels, pat dry the leg of lamb completely. Take a few slits on both sides the leg of lamb and season with salt and black pepper.

Place the leg of lamb onto a wire rack and arrange it onto the top oven rack. Broil for about 5-7 minutes per side.

Remove from the oven and transfer the leg of lamb onto a platter. Now, set the oven temperature to 375 ° F. Arrange a rack in the middle of the oven. Place a wire rack into a large roasting pan.

Insert the garlic slices in the slits of leg of lamb and rub with spice mixture generously.

In a bowl, add the potatoes, onion, garlic powder, paprika and a little salt, and toss to coat well.

Place 2 cups of water into the bottom of the prepared roasting pan. Place the leg of lamb in the middle and arrange the potatoes and onion wedges around the lamb. Roast for about 1 hour.

Remove from the oven and place the leg of lamb onto a cutting board for at least 20 minutes before carving.

Cut into desired sized slices and serve alongside potatoes.

Nutrition: 651 Kcal, Protein 65 g, Carbs 36 g, Fat 18.1 g, Sugars 3.1 g

Lamb Chops with Veggies

Prep **Time:** **20 mins**

Cook Time: 25 mins

Servings: 4

Ingredients:

- *8 (4-ounce) lamb loin chops*
- *½ cup fresh basil leaves*
- *½ cup fresh mint leaves*

- *1 tablespoon fresh rosemary leaves*
- *2 garlic cloves*
- *3 tablespoons olive oil*
- *2 zucchinis, sliced*
- *1 red bell pepper, seeded and cut into large chucks*
- *1 eggplant, sliced*
- *1 ounce feta cheese, crumbled*
- *8 ounces cherry tomatoes*

Instructions

Preheat the oven to 390 degrees F.

In a food processor, add the fresh herbs, garlic and 2 tablespoons of the oil and pulse until smooth.

Transfer the herb mixture into a large bowl. Add the lamb chops and coat with the herb mixture. Refrigerate to marinate for about 2-3 hours.

In the bottom of a large baking sheet, place the zucchini, bell pepper and eggplant slices and drizzle with the remaining oil. Arrange the lamb chops on top in a single layer. Bake for about 20 minutes.

Remove from the oven and transfer the chops onto a platter. Cover the chops to keep warm.

Place the cherry tomatoes into the baking sheet with veggies and top with the feta cheese.

Bake for about 5-7 minutes.

Serve the chops alongside the vegetables.

Nutrition: 543 Kcal, Protein 61 g, Carbs 12.1 g, Fat 17.3 g, Sugars 6.4 g

Braised Lamb with Carrots

Prep Time: 25 mins
  Cook Time: 2 hours 10 mins
Servings: 4

Ingredients:

- *One tablespoon coconut oil*
- *Two pounds lamb shoulder chops*
- *One sliced large onion*
- *Half cup mushrooms*
- *Three sliced cloves of garlic*
- *A quarter tablespoon allspice*
- *One tablespoon smoked paprika*
- *Three to five sprigs of fresh thyme*
- *Two to three branches of fresh rosemary*
- *Half tablespoon salt*
- *Two bay leaves*
- *Half tablespoon freshly ground black pepper*
- *One cup white wine*
- *Two cups chicken broth (no salt added)*
- *One to two cups beef broth*
- *Eight medium carrots (cut diagonally into 2") or mixed root vegetables*
- *One tablespoon Dijon mustard*

Instructions

Preheat the oven to 325 ° F.

Season your lamb with salt and pepper. Heat the coconut oil in a large saucepan over medium-high heat and brown the lamb on each side for about 1-2 minutes. Remove and set aside from the pot.

Add the onions, mushrooms, and garlic to the pot and cook until the onions start to soften for about 3 minutes. Stir in all the spices, paprika, bay leaves, salt & pepper, and add the wine. Add the chicken broth and carrots. Carry it to a boil and let it simmer for about three minutes.

Return the meat to the pot and lay the vegetables and sauce on top. Divide the mustard on top of each shoulder chop and spread it out. Cover with thyme and rosemary sprigs. Apply sufficient beef broth to coat the sides of the lamb with liquid. Cover and roast for 2 hours in the oven.

Remove the meat and serve with the broth and the vegetables.

Nutrition: 301 Kcal, Protein 25.8 g, Carbs 18.4 g, Fat 10.9 g, Sugars 11.2 g

Greek Lamb Salad

Prep   Time: 45 mins
  Cook Time: 5 mins
Servings: 4

Ingredients:

- *Half cup low-fat natural yogurt*
- *Half tablespoon lemon juice*
- *One crushed garlic clove*
- *Half tablespoon ground cumin*
- *1 lb. lamb loin chop, bones removed and fat trimmed*
- *Three tablespoons olive oil*
- *Two tablespoons fresh mint, shredded*
- *3 oz. shredded lettuce*
- *Half chopped fresh cucumber*
- *Three tomatoes, sliced into thin wedges*
- *Half medium sliced red onion*
- *Half cup roughly chopped fresh coriander leaves*
- *Eight pieces of roasted wholegrain bread*

Instructions

Add the yogurt, lemon juice, garlic, and cumin to a tiny mixing bowl to create the dressing. Mix thoroughly.

In a ziploc bag, put one-third of the dressing, add the lamb, seal the bag and give it a good shake to coat the lamb. Marinate the meat in the fridge for a period of 30 minutes.

Save the remainder of the dressing for later in the refrigerator.

Add the olive oil in a non-stick pan over medium heat. Add the lamb and cook on either side for a couple of minutes.

Add more of the mint to the remainder of the dressing.

On each plate, place the salad (lettuce, tomato, cucumber, and onion). Sprinkle the remaining little bit of mint and the cilantro with it. Add the lamb to the salad and drizzle some of the sauce over the whole salad. Serve with two pieces of toast per dishes.

Nutrition: 131 Kcal, Protein 21.8 g, Carbs 8.4 g, Fat 12.1 g

Lamb Stew for Diabetics

Prep **Time:** **20 mins**
   Cook Time: 1 hour 30 mins
Servings: 6

Ingredients:

- *Two medium onions*
- *Four stalks celery*
- *One tablespoon olive oil*
- *One-pound lean stewing lamb*
- *Two cloves' garlic*
- *Three cups water*
- *A quarter cup barley*
- *Two to three bay leaves*
- *Two cups peeled diced rutabagas*
- *One cup peeled diced turnip*
- *One medium peeled and diced carrot*
- *One medium peeled and diced potato*
- *One cup cleaned button mushroom*
- *Nineteen oz can stewed tomatoes*
- *One tablespoon savory salt*
- *One tablespoon paprika*
- *Half tablespoon oregano*
- *Half tablespoon black pepper*
- *One tablespoon Worcestershire sauce*

Instructions

Peel and coarsely cut the onions. Coarsely chop the celery as well. Peel the garlic and mince. Sauté until softened in the oil; stir them into a broad stew pot.

In a frying pan, place the lamb and cook until browned; whisk in the garlic; then add the onions and celery to the meat. Transfer the water, the barley, and the bay leaves to the stew pot.

Peel and cut into bite-sized bits of all the remaining vegetables.

In the order specified, add them to the stew. Then add the spices.

Simmer the stew until the meat will be tender.

Add a little more water as required.

Nutrition: 391 Kcal, Protein 28.9 g, Carbs 32.7 g, Fat 15.9 g, Sugars 10.2 g

Shepherd's Pie

Prep   **Time:**   **20 mins**

           Cook Time: 1 hour

Servings: 2

Ingredients:

- *5 oz. of lean minced lamb*
- *One chopped onion*
- *Two peeled and grated carrots*
- *A pinch of cinnamon*
- *A pinch of mixed herbs*
- *Two tablespoons plain flour*
- *One tablespoon Worcestershire sauce*
- *¾ cup beef stock*
- *One tablespoon oil*
- *One finely sliced leek*
- *14 oz. of peeled and chopped potatoes*
- *Two tablespoons milk*
- *Two tablespoons grated Parmesan*

Instructions

Put a non-stick pan with the lamb, onion, and carrot, and cook for 5-6 minutes until the lamb is browned. Drain the extra fat. Add the cinnamon, herbs, flour, Worcestershire sauce, bring to a boil, and simmer 10 minutes gently.

In a small skillet, heat the oil, add the leeks, and fry for 3-4 minutes. Preheat the oven to 400 ° F.

Put the potatoes in a boiling water pan and simmer until tender, for 12-15 minutes. Then drain and mash. Add the milk and leeks.

Spoon the meat into a medium oven-proof dish and smooth over the potato and leek mixture then sprinkle over the Parmesan.

Cook into the oven for 20-30 minutes, until golden.

Nutrition: 273 Kcal, Protein 18.6 g, Carbs 31.6 g, Fat 7.2 g, Sugars 7.9 g

FISH AND SEAFOOD RECIPES

Mediterranean Baked Fish

Prep Time: **15 mins**

Cook Time: 30 mins

Servings: 4

Ingredients:

- *Two courgettes, trimmed, sliced into chunks*
- *Two Lebanese eggplants, trimmed, sliced into chunks*
- *6 oz. capsicums, halved, seeded*

- *One thickly sliced red onion*
- *Two sliced garlic cloves*
- *Lemon juice*
- *One tablespoon olive oil*
- *14 oz. of can diced tomatoes*
- *A quarter cup Kalamata olives*
- *A quarter cup parsley leaves*
- *A quarter cup dill, chopped*
- *Four pieces firm white fish fillets (6 oz. each one)*
- *One tablespoon of toasted pine nuts*
- *Couscous and lemon wedges for serving*

Instructions

Preheat the oven to 350 ° F. Using olive oil to spray a broad baking dish.

Combine the courgettes, eggplants, capsicums, ginger, garlic, and zest. Hey, season. Pour more than half of the juice and oil together. Bake for 10-15 minutes.

Stir vegetables with olives, tomatoes, and half mixture of herbs. Add fish and drizzle with remaining oil.

Bake for 10-15 minutes. Serve with lemon wedges and couscous.

Nutrition: 421 Kcal, Protein 32 g, Carbs 30.2 g, Fat 18 g, Sugars 7.8 g

Herbed Roasted Cod

Prep Time: 10 Minutes

Cook Time: 45 minutes

Servings: 4

Ingredients:

- *4 cod fillets*
- *4 parsley sprigs*
- *2 cilantro sprigs*
- *2 basil sprigs*

- 1 lemon, sliced
- Salt and pepper to taste
- 2 tablespoons olive oil

Instructions:

Season the cod with salt and pepper.

Place the parsley, cilantro, basil and lemon slices at the bottom of a deep dish baking pan.

Place the cod over the herbs and cook in the preheated oven at 350 °F for 15 minutes.

Serve the cod warm and fresh with your favorite side dish.

Nutrition: Calories: 192 Fat: 8.1 g Protein: 28.6 g Carbohydrates: 0.1 g

Fish Soup

Prep Time: 10 minutes   **Cook Time: 20 minutes**

Servings: 4

Ingredients:

- 2 tbsps. olive oil
- 1 tbsp. garlic, minced
- ½ cup tomatoes, crushed
- 1 yellow onion, chopped
- 1 quart of veggie stock
- 1 lb. cod, skinless, boneless and cubed

- ¼ tsp. rosemary, dried
- A pinch of salt and black pepper

Instructions:

Heat up a pot with the oil over medium heat, add the onion and the garlic and sauté for 5 minutes.

Add the rest of the ingredients, toss, simmer over medium heat for 15 minutes more, divide into bowls and serve for lunch.

Nutrition: Calories 198, Fat: 8.1 g, Carbs: 4.2 g, Protein: 26.4 g

Greek Roasted Fish

Prep Time: 5 minutes   **Cook**
Time: 30 minutes
Servings: 4

Ingredients:

- *4 salmon fillets*
- *tablespoon chopped oregano*
- *1 teaspoon dried basil*
- *1 zucchini, sliced*
- *1 red onion, sliced*
- *1 carrot, sliced*
- *1 lemon, sliced*
- *tablespoons extra virgin olive oil*
- *Salt and pepper to taste*

Instructions:
Add all the ingredients in a deep dish baking pan.
Season with salt and pepper and cook in the preheated oven at 350 °F for 20 minutes.

Nutrition: Calories: 328; Fat: 13 g; Protein: 38 g; Carbs: 8 g

Tuna with Olives

Prep Time: 15 minutes   **Cook Time: 14**
minutes
Servings: 4

Ingredients:

- 4 (6-ounce) (1-inch thick) tuna steaks
- 2 tablespoons extra-virgin olive oil, divided
- Salt and ground black pepper, as required
- 2 garlic cloves, minced
- 1 cup fresh tomatoes, chopped
- 1 cup dry white wine
- 2/3 cup green olives, pitted and sliced
- ¼ cup capers, drained
- 2 tablespoons fresh thyme, chopped
- 1½ tablespoons fresh lemon zest, grated
- 2 tablespoons fresh lemon juice
- 3 tablespoons fresh parsley, chopped

Instructions:

Preheat the grill to high heat. Grease the grill grate.

Coat the tuna steaks with 1 tablespoon of the oil and sprinkle with salt and black pepper.

Set aside for about 5 minutes.

For sauce: in a small skillet, heat the remaining oil over medium heat and sauté the garlic for about 1 minute. Add the tomatoes and cook for about 2 minutes. Stir in the wine and bring to a boil. Add the remaining ingredients except the parsley and cook, uncovered for about 5 minutes.

Stir in the parsley, salt and black pepper and remove from the heat.

Meanwhile, grill the tuna steaks over direct heat for about 1-2 minutes per side.

Serve the tuna steaks hot with the topping of sauce.

Nutrition: Calories 468, Fat 20.4 g, Carbs 7.3 g, Sugar 2 g, Protein 52.1 g

Stuffed Swordfish

Prep Time: 15 minutes
Time: 14 minutes
Servings: 2

Cook

Ingredients:

- *1 (8-ounce) (2-inch thick) swordfish steak*
- *1½ tablespoons olive oil, divided*
- *1 tablespoon fresh lemon juice*
- *2 cups fresh spinach, torn into bite size pieces*
- *1 garlic clove, minced*
- *¼ cup feta cheese, crumbled*

Instructions:
Preheat the outdoor grill to high heat. Lightly, grease the grill grate.
Carefully, cut a slit on one side of fish steak to create a pocket.
In a bowl, add 1 tablespoon of the oil and lemon juice and mix.
Coat the both sides of fish with oil mixture evenly.
In a small skillet, add the remaining oil and garlic over medium heat and cook until heated. Add the spinach and cook for about 2-3 minutes or until wilted.
Remove from the heat.
Stuff the fish pocket with spinach, followed by the feta cheese. Grill the fish pocket for about 8 minutes.
Flip and cook for about 5-6 minutes or until desired doneness of fish.
Cut the fish pocket into 2 equal sized pieces and serve.

Nutrition: Calories 296, Fat 17 g, Carbs 2.5 g, Sugar 1.1 g, Protein 32.5 g

Shrimp Zoodles

Prep Time: 10 minutes
minutes
Servings: 4

Cook Time: 5

Ingredients:

- 2 zucchini, spiralized
- 1 lb shrimp, peeled and deveined
- 1/2 tsp paprika
- 1 tbsp basil, chopped
- 1/2 lemon juice
- 1 tsp garlic, minced
- 2 tbsp olive oil
- 1 cup vegetable stock
- Pepper
- Salt

Instructions:

Add oil into the inner pot of instant pot and set the pot on sauté mode. Add garlic and sauté for a minute. Add shrimp and lemon juice and stir well and cook for 1 minute. Add remaining ingredients and stir well.

Seal pot with lid and cook on high for 3 minutes.

Once done, release pressure using quick release. Remove lid.

Nutrition: Calories 215, Fat 9.2 g, Carbs 5.8 g, Sugar 2 g, Protein 27.3 g

Simple Lemon Clams

Prep Time: 10 minutes   **Cook Time: 10**
minutes
Servings: 4

Ingredients:

- 1 lb clams, clean
- 1 tbsp fresh lemon juice
- 1 lemon zest, grated
- 1 onion, chopped
- 1/2 cup fish stock

- *Pepper*
- *Salt*

Instructions:

Add all ingredients into the inner pot of instant pot and stir well.
Seal pot with lid and cook on high for 10 minutes.
Once done, release pressure using quick release. Remove lid.

Nutrition: Calories 76, Fat 0.6 g, Carbs 16.4 g, Protein 1.8 g

Seafood Stew

Prep Time: 20 minutes   **Cook Time: 25 minutes**
Servings: 6

Ingredients:

- *2 tablespoons olive oil*
- *1 medium onion, chopped finely*
- *2 garlic cloves, minced*
- *¼ teaspoon red pepper flakes, crushed*
- *½ pound plum tomatoes, seeded and chopped*
- *1/3 cup white wine*
- *1 cup clam juice*
- *1 tablespoon tomato paste*
- *Salt, as required*
- *1-pound snapper fillets, cubed into 1-inch size*
- *1-pound large shrimp, peeled and deveined*
- *½ pound sea scallops*
- *1/3 cup fresh parsley, minced*
- *1 teaspoon fresh lemon zest, grated finely*

Instructions:

In a large Dutch oven, heat oil over medium heat and sauté the onion for about 3-4 minutes. Add the garlic and red pepper flakes and sauté for about 1 minute. Add the tomatoes and cook for about 2 minutes.

Stir in the wine, clam juice, tomato paste and salt and bring to a boil. Reduce the heat to low and simmer, covered for about 10 minutes. Stir in the seafood and simmer, covered for about 6-8 minutes. Stir in the parsley and remove from heat.

Serve hot with the garnishing of lemon zest.

Nutrition: Calories 313, Fat 7.8 g, Carbs 11.6 g, Sugar 4.1 g, Protein 44.3 g

Pesto Fish Fillet

Prep Time: 10 minutes   **Cook Time: 8 minutes**
Servings: 4

Ingredients:

- *4 halibut fillets*
- *1/2 cup water*
- *1 tbsp lemon zest, grated*
- *1 tbsp capers*
- *1/2 cup basil, chopped*
- *1 tbsp garlic, chopped*
- *1 avocado, peeled and chopped*
- *Pepper*
- *Salt*

Instructions:
Add lemon zest, capers, basil, garlic, avocado, pepper, and salt into the blender blend until smooth.

Place fish fillets on aluminum foil and spread a blended mixture on fish fillets.

Fold foil around the fish fillets.

Pour water into the instant pot and place trivet in the pot.

Place foil fish packet on the trivet.
Seal pot with lid and cook on high for 8 minutes.
Once done, allow to release pressure naturally. Remove lid.

Nutrition: Calories 426, Fat 16.6 g, Carbs 5.5 g, Sugar 0.4 g, Protein 61.8 g

Salmon with Broccoli

Prep Time: 10 minutes   **Cook Time: 4 minutes**
Servings: 4

Ingredients:

- *4 salmon fillets*
- *10 oz broccoli florets*
- *1 1/2 cups water*
- *1 tbsp olive oil*
- *Pepper*
- *Salt*

Instructions:
Pour water into the instant pot then place steamer basket in the pot.
Place salmon in the steamer basket and season with pepper and salt and drizzle with oil.
Add broccoli on top of salmon in the steamer basket.
Seal pot with lid and cook on high for 4 minutes.
Once done, release pressure using quick release. Remove lid.

Nutrition: Calories 290, Fat 14.7 g, Carbs 4.7 g, Sugar 1.2 g, Protein 36.5 g

Healthy Carrot & Shrimp

Prep Time: 10 minutes   **Cook
Time: 6 minutes**
Servings: 4

Ingredients:

- *1 lb shrimp, peeled and deveined*
- *1 tbsp chives, chopped*
- *1 onion, chopped*
- *1 tbsp olive oil*
- *1 cup fish stock*
- *1 cup carrots, sliced*
- *Pepper*
- *Salt*

Instructions:

Add oil into the inner pot of instant pot and set the pot on sauté mode. Add onion and sauté for 2 minutes. Add remaining ingredients and stir well.

Seal pot with lid and cook on high for 4 minutes.

Once done, release pressure using quick release. Remove lid.

Nutrition: Calories 197, Fat 5.9 g, Carbs 7 g, Sugar 2.5 g, Protein 27.7 g

Cumin-Crusted Fish Fillets

Prep   **Time:**   **15
mins**
        Cook Time: 30 mins
Servings: 4

Ingredients:

- *Two tablespoons ground cumin*
- *One quarter tablespoon thyme*
- *One tablespoon paprika*

- *Half tablespoon lemon pepper*
- *One-pound white fish fillets (like halibut, or cod)*
- *Half tablespoon canola oil*

- *Lemon*
- *Two tablespoons chopped parsley*

Instructions

Mix the cumin, thyme, paprika, and lemon pepper together in a shallow dish. Rub the combination of spices on each side of the fillets.

Heat canola oil in a wide skillet placed over medium heat. Add fish fillets and cook until browned on all sides.

Sprinkle with parsley and serve right away with wedges of lemon.

Nutrition: 131 Kcal, Protein 21 g, Carbs 1 g, Fat 3.4 g

Lemon and Parmesan Fish

Prep **Time:** **15 mins**

Cook Time: 25 mins

Servings: 2

Ingredients:

- *Two ounces frozen sole fillets*
- *Cooking spray*
- *Two tablespoons grated Parmesan cheese*
- *Two tablespoons butter, melted*
- *Half tablespoon lemon peel, finely shredded*

- *One eighth tablespoon ground black pepper*
- *One Lemon wedge*

Instructions

Preheat the oven to 450 ° F.

Thaw fish and rinse.

Cover a shallow baking pan with cooking spray. Starting from the ends, roll up the fish fillets. Combine parmesan cheese, melted butter, lemon peel, and pepper in a shallow dish. Use fingertips to gently push breadcrumbs into fish.

Bake into the oven for 6 minutes.

Nutrition: 190 Kcal, Protein 24 g, Carbs 6.8 g, Fat 6.9 g, Sugars 0.5 g

Mediterranean Fish Fillets

Prep Time: 10 minutes

Cook Time: 3 minutes

Servings: 4

Ingredients:

- *4 cod fillets*
- *1 lb grape tomatoes, halved*
- *1 cup olives, pitted and sliced*
- *2 tbsp capers*
- *1 tsp dried thyme*
- *2 tbsp olive oil*
- *1 tsp garlic, minced*
- *Pepper*
- *Salt*

Instructions:

Pour 1 cup water into the instant pot then place steamer rack in the pot.

Spray heat-safe baking dish with cooking spray.

Add half grape tomatoes into the dish and season with pepper and salt.

Arrange fish fillets on top of cherry tomatoes. Drizzle with oil and season with garlic, thyme, capers, pepper, and salt. Spread olives and remaining grape tomatoes on top of fish fillets.

Place dish on top of steamer rack in the pot.

Seal pot with a lid and select manual and cook on high for 3 minutes.

Once done, release pressure using quick release. Remove lid.

Nutrition: Calories 212, Fat 11.9 g, Carbs 7.1 g, Sugar 3 g, Protein 21.4 g

Creamy Fish Stew

Prep Time: 10 minutes   **Cook Time: 8 minutes**
Servings: 6

Ingredients:

- 1 lb white fish fillets, cut into chunks
- 2 tbsp olive oil
- 1 cup kale, chopped
- 1 cup cauliflower, chopped
- 1 cup broccoli, chopped
- 3 cups fish broth
- 1 cup heavy cream
- 2 celery stalks, diced
- 1 carrot, sliced
- 1 onion, diced
- Pepper
- Salt

Instructions:

Add oil into the inner pot of instant pot and set the pot on sauté mode. Add onion and sauté for 3 minutes. Add remaining ingredients except for heavy cream and stir well.

Seal pot with lid and cook on high for 5 minutes.
Once done, allow to release pressure naturally. Remove lid.
Stir in heavy cream and serve.

Nutrition: Calories 296, Fat 19.3 g, Carbs 7.5 g, Sugar 2.6 g, Protein 22.8 g

Salmon Stew

Prep Time: 10 minutes   **Cook Time: 8 minutes**
Servings: 6

Ingredients:

- *2 lbs salmon fillet, cubed*
- *1 onion, chopped*
- *2 cups fish broth*
- *1 tbsp olive oil*
- *Pepper*
- *salt*

Instructions:
Add oil into the inner pot of instant pot and set the pot on sauté mode. Add onion and sauté for 2 minutes. Add remaining ingredients and stir well.
Seal pot with lid and cook on high for 6 minutes.
Once done, release pressure using quick release. Remove lid.
Stir and serve.

Nutrition: Calories 243, Fat 12.6 g, Carbs 0.8 g, Sugar 0.3 g, Protein 31 g

Feta Tomato Sea Bass

Prep Time: 10 minutes
Time: 8 minutes
Servings: 4

Ingredients:

- *4 sea bass fillets*
- *1 1/2 cups water*
- *1 tbsp olive oil*

- *1 tsp garlic, minced*
- *1 tsp basil, chopped*

- *1 tsp parsley, chopped*
- *1/2 cup feta cheese, crumbled*
- *1 cup can tomatoes, diced*
- *Pepper*
- *Salt*

Instructions:
Season fish fillets with pepper and salt.
Pour 2 cups of water into the instant pot then place steamer rack in the pot.
Place fish fillets on steamer rack in the pot. Seal pot with lid and cook on high for 5 minutes.
Once done, release pressure using quick release. Remove lid.
Remove fish fillets from the pot and clean the pot.
Add oil into the inner pot of instant pot and set the pot on sauté mode. Add garlic and sauté for 1 minute. Add tomatoes, parsley, and basil and stir well and cook for 1 minute. Add fish fillets and top with crumbled cheese and cook for a minute.

Nutrition: Calories 219, Fat 10.1 g, Carbs 4 g, Sugar 2.8 g, Protein 27.1 g

Flavors Codfish with Shrimp

Prep Time: 10 minutes
Time: 5 minutes
Servings: 6

Ingredients:

- 1 lb codfish, cut into chunks
- 1 1/2 lbs shrimp
- 28 oz can tomatoes, diced
- 1 cup dry white wine
- 1 bay leaf
- 1 tsp cayenne
- 1 tsp oregano
- 1 shallot, chopped
- 1 tsp garlic, minced
- 1 tbsp olive oil
- 1/2 tsp salt

Instructions:

Add oil into the inner pot of instant pot and set the pot on sauté mode. Add shallot and garlic and sauté for 2 minutes. Add wine, bay leaf, cayenne, oregano, and salt and cook for 3 minutes. Add remaining ingredients and stir well.

Seal pot with a lid and select manual and cook on low for 0 minutes. Once done, release pressure using quick release. Remove lid.

Nutrition: Calories 281, Fat 5 g, Carbs 10.5 g, Sugar 4.9 g, Protein 40.7 g

Garlicky Shrimp

Prep Time: 15 minutes

Cook Time: 6 minutes

Servings: 4

Ingredients:

- *2 tablespoons olive oil*
- *3 garlic cloves, sliced*
- *1-pound shrimp, peeled and deveined*
- *1 tablespoon fresh rosemary, chopped*
- *½ teaspoon red pepper flakes, crushed*
- *Salt and ground black pepper, as required*
- *1 tablespoon fresh lemon juice*

Instructions:

In a large skillet, heat the oil over medium heat and sauté the garlic slices or about 2 minutes or until golden brown.

With a slotted spoon, transfer the garlic slices into a bowl.

In the same skillet, add the shrimp, rosemary, red pepper flakes. salt and black pepper and cook for about 3-4 minutes, stirring frequently.

Stir in the lemon juice and remove from the heat.

Serve hot with a topping of the garlic slices.

Nutrition: Calories 202, Fat 9.1 g, Carbs 3.2 g, Sugar 0.1 g

Diabetic Oven-Fried Fish & Chips

Prep   **Time:**   **15 mins**

Cook Time: 45 mins

Servings: 4

Ingredients:

- *Cooking spray*
- *Half pound potatoes, scrubbed and sliced into quarter-inch-thick wedges*

- *Half tablespoon Cajun seasoning, divided*
- *One-quarter cup all-purpose flour*

- *One quarter tablespoon salt*

- *One pound cod*
- *Four tablespoons canola oil*
- *Two large egg whites, beaten*

Instructions

Preheat the oven to 425 ° F.

Cover 2 broad baking sheets with cooking spray.

Place the potatoes in a big bowl and mix with oil, and 3/4 tsp of Cajun seasoning. Spread them on the baking sheet. Bake on the lower rack of the oven from 30 to 35 minutes, rotating the potatoes every 10 minutes.

Meanwhile, in a shallow dish, put flour, the remaining Cajun seasoning, and salt. In another shallow dish beat the egg whites. Dredge the cod in the white egg, and then in the flour. Place it on the baking sheets that was prepared. Cover both sides with cooking spray on the breaded cod.

Bake the fish around 20 minutes, until the breading is golden brown.

Lemon Grilled Fish on Grilled Asparagus

Prep   Time: 15 mins

Cook Time: 45 mins

Servings: 4

Ingredients:

- *14 oz. asparagus spears (ends trimmed)*
- *Four cod fillets (4 oz each, rinsed and patted dry)*
- *Juice of one medium lemon*
- *A quarter cup canola oil*
- *A quarter tsp black pepper*
- *Lemon zest*
- *A quarter tsp salt*

Instructions

Coat with cooking spray on the asparagus and steam for 6-8 minutes or until tender-crisp, turning periodically. Set aside and keep warm covered on a rimmed serving platter.

Coat with cooking spray all sides of the cod, sprinkle with black pepper, and cook 3 minutes on either side.

Meanwhile, in a small dish, mix the canola oil, lemon zest, and salt. Spoon the combination of oil over the asparagus. Place the fish on top and squeeze the lemon juice.

Nutrition: 155 Kcal, Protein 22 g, Carbs 5 g, Fat 5.2 g, Sugars 2 g

Trout and Shrimps in Tomato Sauce

Prep   **Time:**   **15 mins**

Cook Time: 15 mins

Servings: 2

Ingredients:

- *Eight oz frozen skinless trout*
- *Six oz frozen shrimp*
- *Two stalks celery, sliced*
- *one-third cup chopped onion*
- *2 tablespoons olive oil*
- *Half tablespoon minced garlic*
- *One cup low-sodium chicken broth*
- *A quarter cup dry white wine*
- *One can drained, no-salt-added diced tomatoes*
- *One can no-salt-added tomato sauce*
- *One eighth tablespoon ground black pepper*
- *Four sprigs of fresh basil*
- *One tablespoon dried oregano*
- *A quarter tablespoon salt*

Instructions

Cut the trout into 1-half-inch bits. Cut the shrimp lengthwise in two. Cover all, and put in the fridge.

Combine onion, celery, and garlic with a wide saucepan with olive oil. Add broth and wine steadily. Bring it to a boil; reduce the heat. Simmer uncovered for 5 minutes.

Stir the oregano, basil, tomato sauce, salt, pepper, and tomatoes. Bring to a boil again; minimize fire. Cover for 5 minutes and simmer. Add the shrimps and trout. Cover and boil for 3 to 5 minutes.

Cod Fillets Adobo

Prep **Time:** **25 mins**

Cook Time: 5 mins

Servings: 4

Ingredients:

- *Two tablespoons olive oil*
- *Two tablespoons lemon juice*
- *Three quarter tablespoons paprika*
- *Three-quarter tablespoons dried oregano*
- *A quarter tablespoon ground cumin*
- *A quarter tablespoon salt*
- *One-eighth tablespoon black pepper*
- *Four cod fillets*

Instructions

In a shallow dish, combine the oil, lemon juice, paprika, oregano, cumin, salt, and pepper. Spread out on both sides of the fish. Put the fish in a dish, cover, and refrigerate for around 20 minutes.

Preheat the broiler.

Place the fish in a broiler-proof baking pan. Broil for 5-7 minutes or before the fish starts to flake.

Nutrition: 201 Kcal, Protein 41 g, Carbs 1 g, Fat 3.4 g, Sugars 0.2 g

Greek-Style Roast Cod

Prep   **Time:**   **15 mins**

           Cook Time: 50 mins

Servings: 2

Ingredients:

- *14 oz. small Lower Carb Potatoes, scrubbed, sliced into wedges*
- *One sliced onion*
- *Two chopped cloves garlic*
- *Half tablespoon dried oregano*
- *Two tablespoons olive oil*
- *Half lemon, cut into thin wedges*
- *Two large tomatoes, cut into wedges*
- *5 oz. cop fillets*
- *Small handful parsley, chopped*

Instructions

Preheat the (fan-forced) oven to 350 ° F. Line a roasting pan with paper for baking. In a dish, incorporate the potatoes, onion, garlic, oregano, and oil. Toss well. Spread it on a single layer out in the pan.

Roast for 15 minutes, turn over the vegetables, and roast for 15 more minutes. To the pan, add the lemon and tomatoes. Bake for 10 minutes. Add the fish fillets to the top and simmer for another 10 minutes. Serve scattering with the parsley.

Nutrition: 371 Kcal, Protein 22 g, Carbs 21 g, Fat 12.1 g, Sugars 8 g

Greek Salmon Bowl

Prep   **Time:**   **30 mins**

Cook Time: 45 mins
Servings: 4

Ingredients:

- One lb. salmon fillet
- Half tablespoon salt, divided
- A quarter tablespoon ground pepper
- Eight oz string beans, trimmed and cut into 1-inch pieces
- Three quarter cup quinoa
- Three quarter cups water
- Three tablespoons lemon juice
- Two tablespoons olive oil
- One minced clove garlic
- Two tablespoons chopped fresh oregano for garnish
- One medium tomato, seeded and chopped
- A quarter cup crumbled feta cheese
- A quarter cup pitted Kalamata olive, halved or sliced

Instructions

Preheat the oven to 400 ° F.

On a baking sheet, position the salmon and sprinkle with 1/8 tsp. Pepper and salt. Bake until the salmon flakes easily, from 20 to 25 minutes.

Meanwhile, in a medium saucepan equipped with a steamer basket, put 1 inch of water to a boil. Add string beans; cover and cook for around 5 minutes until tender-crisp. Put aside.

In a saucepan, combine the quinoa, water, and 1/8 tsp. salt; carry to a simmer. Reduce the heat to medium, cover, and simmer for 15 to 20 minutes before the quinoa is soft, and most of the liquid is absorbed. Fluff with a fork.

Whisk together lemon juice, oil, garlic, oregano, and the remaining quarter tsp of salt in a shallow bowl.

Divide the quinoa into 4 dinner bowls. Over the quinoa, layer the salmon, string beans, tomatoes, feta, and olives. Drizzle with the dressing and garnish, with fresh oregano.

Nutrition: 389 Kcal, Protein 29 g, Carbs 24 g, Fat 21 g, Sugars 3 g

Salmon Sliders with Tangy Mustard Slaw

Prep **Time:** **10**
mins
            Cook Time: 10 mins
Servings: 4

Ingredients:

Slaw

- *One tablespoon spicy brown mustard*
- *One tablespoon canola oil*
- *One tablespoon white vinegar*
- *One quarter tablespoon ground pepper*
- *One cup shredded red cabbage*
- *One small fennel, cored and thinly sliced*

Salad

- *One-quarter cup low-fat plain Greek yogurt*
- *Two tablespoons lemon juice*
- *One tablespoon chopped fresh dill*
- *One quarter tablespoon salt*
- *One eighth tablespoon ground pepper*
- *Two medium carrots, peeled and thinly sliced*
- *One thinly sliced medium cucumber*

Salmon

- *One and a half lb. salmon fillet, skin-on*
- *One quarter tablespoon salt*
- *One quarter tablespoon ground pepper*
- *One tablespoon olive oil*
- *Eight slider buns*

Instructions

Slaw preparation: In a bowl, whisk mustard, oil, vinegar, and a quarter tsp. pepper. Add fennel and cabbage; toss to coat and set aside.

For salad preparation: In another bowl, whisk together yogurt, lemon juice, dill, salt, and 1/8 tsp. pepper. Add the cucumber and carrots; mix to blend.

To cook salmon: Season salmon with salt and pepper. Split it in half if the fillet is too big to fit in the skillet. Heat oil over medium-high heat in a wide cast-iron or nonstick skillet. Add the salmon and cook for 4 minutes. Flip and cook for 5 minutes, depending on the thickness, before the salmon flakes with a fork.

Divide the salmon among buns and top with the slaw. On the side, serve the salad.

Nutrition: 510 Kcal, Protein 40 g, Carbs 34 g, Fat 22 g, Sugars 10 g

Avocados Stuffed with Salmon

Prep Time: 5 minutes   **Cook Time: 5 minutes**
Servings: 2

Ingredients:

- *Avocado (pitted and halved): 1*
- *Olive oil: 2 tablespoons*
- *Lemon juice: 1*
- *Smoked salmon (flaked): 2 ounces*
- *Goat cheese (crumbled): 1 ounce*
- *Salt and black pepper*

Instructions:

Combine the salmon with lemon juice, oil, cheese, salt, and pepper in your food processor and pulsate well.

Divide this mixture into avocado halves and serve.

Nutrition: Calories: 300; Fat: 15 g; Carbs: 8 g; Protein: 16 g

Tilapia and Herb Sauce

Prep Time: 15 mins

Cook Time: 15 mins

Servings: 4

Ingredients:

- *14-ounce cans diced tomatoes with basil and garlic, undrained*
- *1/3 cup fresh parsley, chopped and divided*
- *¼ teaspoon dried oregano*
- *½ teaspoon red pepper flakes, crushed*
- *6-ounce tilapia fillets*
- *2 tablespoons fresh lemon juice*
- *2/3 cup feta cheese, crumbled*

Instructions

Preheat the oven to 400 ° F.

In a shallow baking dish, add the tomatoes, ¼ cup of parsley, oregano and red pepper flakes, and mix.

Arrange the tilapia fillets over the tomato mixture in a single layer and drizzle with the lemon juice. Sprinkle with the feta cheese.

Bake for about 12-14 minutes.

Serve hot with the remaining parsley.

Nutrition: 245 Kcal, Protein 36 g, Carbs 9 g, Fat 6.5 g, Sugars 5.4 g

AIR FRY RECIPES

Salmon Cakes in Air Fryer

Prep   **Time:**   **10 mins**

            Cook Time: 10 mins

Servings: 2

Ingredients:

- *Fresh salmon fillet 8 oz.*
- *Egg 1*
- *Salt 1/8 tsp*
- *Garlic powder ¼ tsp*
- *Sliced lemon 1*

Instructions:

In the bowl, chop the salmon, add the egg & spices.

Form tiny cakes.

Let the Air fryer preheat to 390. On the bottom of the air fryer bowl lay sliced lemons—place cakes on top.

Cook them for seven minutes. Based on your diet preferences, eat with your chosen dip.

Nutrition: 194 Kcal, Protein 25 g, Carbs 1 g, Fat 9 g

Coconut Shrimp

Prep   **Time:**   **10 mins**

            Cook Time: 30 mins

Servings: 4

Ingredients:

- *Pork Rinds: ½ cup (Crushed)*
- *Jumbo Shrimp:4 cups. (deveined)*
- *Coconut Flakes preferably: ½ cup*
- *Eggs: two*
- *Flour of coconut: ½ cup*
- *Any oil of your choice for frying at least half-inch in pan*
- *Freshly ground black pepper & kosher salt to taste*

Dipping sauce (Pina colada flavor)

- *Powdered Sugar as Substitute: 2-3 tablespoon*
- *Mayonnaise: 3 tablespoons*
- *Sour Cream: ½ cup*
- *Coconut Extract or to taste: ¼ tsp*
- *Coconut Cream: 3 tablespoons*
- *Pineapple Flavoring as much to taste: ¼ tsp*
- *Coconut Flakes preferably unsweetened this is optional: 3 tablespoons*

Instructions:

Pina Colada (Sauce):

Mix all the ingredients into a tiny bowl for the Dipping sauce (Pina colada flavor). Combine well and put in the fridge until ready to serve.

Shrimps:

Whip all eggs in a deep bowl, and a small, shallow bowl, add the crushed pork rinds, coconut flour, sea salt, coconut flakes, and freshly ground black pepper.

Put the shrimp one by one in the mixed eggs for dipping, then in the coconut flour blend. Put them on a clean plate or put them on your air fryer's basket.

Place the shrimp battered in a single layer on your air fryer basket. Spritz the shrimp with oil and cook for 8-10 minutes at 360 ° F, flipping them through halfway.

Enjoy hot with dipping sauce.

Nutrition: 340 Kcal, Protein 25 g, Carbs 9 g, Fat 16 g

Crispy Fish Sticks in Air Fryer

Prep   **Time:**   **10 mins**

                 Cook Time: 15 mins

Servings: 4

Ingredients:

- *Whitefish such as cod 1 lb.*
- *Mayonnaise ¼ c*
- *Dijon mustard 2 tbsp.*
- *Water 2 tbsp.*
- *Pork rind 1&1/2 c*
- *Cajun seasoning ¾ tsp*
- *Kosher salt& pepper to taste*

Instructions

Spray non-stick cooking spray to the air fryer rack.

Pat the fish dry & cut into sticks about 1 inch by 2 inches' broad

Stir together the mayo, mustard, and water in a tiny small dish. Mix the pork rinds & Cajun seasoning into another small container.

Adding kosher salt& pepper to taste (both pork rinds & seasoning can have a decent amount of kosher salt, so you can dip a finger to see how salty it is).

Working for one slice of fish at a time, dip to cover in the mayo mix & then tap off the excess. Dip into the mixture of pork rind, then flip to cover. Place on the rack of an air fryer.

Set at 400F to Air Fry & bake for 5 minutes, then turn the fish with tongs and bake for another 5 minutes. Serve.

Nutritional value: 263 Kcal, Protein 26.4 g, Carbs 1 g, Fat 16 g

Basil-Parmesan Crusted Salmon

Prep   **Time:**   **5**
mins

                    Cook Time: 15 mins

Servings: 4

Ingredients:

- *Grated Parmesan: 3 tablespoons*
- *Skinless four salmon fillets*
- *Salt: 1/4 teaspoon*

- *Freshly ground black pepper*
- *Low-fat mayonnaise: 3 tablespoons*

- *Basil leaves, chopped*
- *Half lemon*

Instructions:

Let the air fryer preheat to 400F. Spray the basket with olive oil.

With salt, pepper, and lemon juice, season the salmon.

In a bowl, mix two tablespoons of Parmesan cheese with mayonnaise and basil leaves.

Add this mix and more parmesan on top of salmon and cook for seven minutes or until fully cooked.

Nutrition: 289 Kcal, Protein 30 g, Carbs 1.5 g, Fat 18.5 g

Cajun Shrimp in Air Fryer

Prep   **Time:**   **10**
mins

                    Cook Time: 20 mins

Servings: 4

Ingredients:

- *Peeled, 24 extra-jumbo shrimp*
- *Olive oil: 2 tablespoons*
- *Cajun seasoning: 1 tablespoon*
- *one zucchini, thick slices (half-moons)*
- *Cooked Turkey: ¼ cup*
- *Yellow squash, sliced half-moons*
- *Kosher salt: 1/4 teaspoon*

Instructions:

In a bowl, mix the shrimp with Cajun seasoning.

In another bowl, add zucchini, turkey, salt, squash, and coat with oil.

Let the air fryer preheat to 400F

Move the shrimp and vegetable mix to the fryer basket and cook for three minutes.

Nutrition: 284 Kcal, Protein 31 g, Carbs 8 g, Fat 14 g

Crispy Air Fryer Fish

Prep   **Time:**   **10 mins**

         Cook Time: 17 mins

Servings: 4

Ingredients:

- *Old bay: 2 tsp*
- *4-6, cut in half, Whiting Fish fillets*
- *Fine cornmeal: ¾ cup*

- *Flour: ¼ cup*
- *Paprika: 1 tsp*
- *Garlic powder: half tsp*
- *Salt: 1 and ½ tsp*
- *Freshly ground black pepper: half tsp*

Instructions:
In a ziploc bag, add all ingredients and coat the fish fillets with it.
Spray oil on the basket of air fryer and put the fish in it.
Cook for ten minutes at 400 F. flip fish if necessary and coat with oil spray and cook for another seven-minute.
Serve with salad green.

Nutrition: 254 Kcal, Protein 17.5 g, Carbs 8.2g, Fat 12.7 g

Air Fryer Lemon Cod

Prep   **Time:**   **5 mins**
               Cook Time: 10 mins
Servings: 1

Ingredients:

- *One cod fillet*
- *Dried parsley*
- *Kosher salt and pepper to taste*
- *Garlic powder*
- *One lemon*

Instructions:
In a bowl, mix all ingredients and coat the fish fillet with spices.
Slice the lemon and lay at the bottom of the air fryer basket.
Put spiced fish on top. Cover the fish with lemon slices.
Cook for ten minutes at 375F, the internal temperature of fish should be 145F.
Serve with microgreen salad.

Nutrition: 101 Kcal, Protein 16 g, Carbs 10 g, Fat 1 g

Air Fryer Salmon Fillets

Prep   **Time:**   **5**
mins

              Cook Time: 15 mins

Servings: 2

Ingredients:

- *Low-fat Greek yogurt: 1/4 cup*
- *Two salmon fillets*
- *Fresh dill: 1 tbsp. (chopped)*
- *One lemon and lemon juice*
- *Garlic powder: half tsp.*
- *Kosher salt and pepper*

Instructions:

Cut the lemon in slices and lay at the bottom of the air fryer basket.
Season the salmon with kosher salt and pepper. Put salmon on top of lemons.
Let it cook at 330 degrees for 15 minutes.
In the meantime, mix garlic powder, lemon juice, salt, pepper with yogurt and dill.
Serve the fish with sauce.

Nutritional value: 194 Kcal, Carbs 6 g, Protein 25 g , Fat 7 g

Air Fryer Fish & Chips

Prep   **Time:**   **10**
mins

              Cook Time: 35 mins

Servings: 4

Ingredients:

- *4 cups of any fish fillet*
- *flour: 1/4 cup*

- *Whole wheat breadcrumbs: one cup*
- *One egg*
- *Oil: 2 tbsp.*
- *Potatoes*
- *Salt: 1 tsp.*

Instructions:

Cut the potatoes in fries. Then coat with oil and salt.

Cook in the air fryer for 20 minutes at 400 F, toss the fries halfway through.

In the meantime, coat fish in flour, then in the whisked egg, and finally in breadcrumbs mix.

Place the fish in the air fryer and let it cook at 330F for 15 minutes.

Flip it halfway through, if needed.

Serve with tartar sauce and salad green.

Nutrition: 409 Kcal, Carbs 44 g, Protein 30 g, Fat 11 g

Grilled Salmon with Lemon

Prep   **Time:**   **10 mins**

                 Cook Time: 20 mins

Servings: 4

Ingredients:

- *Olive oil: 2 tablespoons*
- *Two Salmon fillets*
- *Lemon juice*
- *Water: 1/3 cup*
- *Gluten-free light soy sauce: 1/3 cup*
- *Scallion slices*
- *Cherry tomato*
- *Freshly ground black pepper, garlic powder, kosher salt to taste*

Instructions:

Season salmon with pepper and salt

In a bowl, mix soy sauce, lemon juice, water, oil. Add salmon in this marinade and let it rest for least two hours.

Let the air fryer preheat at 356°F

Place fish in the air fryer and cook for 8 minutes.

Move to a dish and top with scallion slices.

Nutrition: 211 Kcal, Protein 15 g, Carbs 4.9 g, Fat 9 g

Air-Fried Fish Nuggets

Prep Time: 15 mins

Cook Time: 10 mins

Servings: 4

Ingredients:

- *Fish fillets in cubes: 2 cups(skinless)*
- *1 egg, beaten*
- *Flour: 5 tablespoons*

- *Water: 5 tablespoons*
- *Kosher salt and pepper to taste*
- *Breadcrumbs mix*
- *Smoked paprika: 1 tablespoon*
- *Whole wheat breadcrumbs: ¼ cup*
- *Garlic powder: 1 tablespoon*

Instructions:

Season the fish cubes with kosher salt and pepper.

In a bowl, add flour and gradually add water, mixing as you add.

Then mix in the egg. And keep mixing but do not over mix.

Coat the cubes in batter, then in the breadcrumb mix. Coat well

Place the cubes in a baking tray and spray with oil.

Let the air fryer preheat to 392 F.
Place cubes in the air fryer and cook for 12 minutes or until well cooked and golden brown.
Serve with salad greens.

Nutrition: 184.2 Kcal, Protein 1 9 g, Carb 10 g, Fat 3.3 g

Garlic Rosemary Grilled Prawns

Prep   Time: 5 mins

Cook Time: 10 mins

Servings: 2

Ingredients:

- *Melted butter: 1/2 tbsp.*
- *Green capsicum: slices*
- *Eight prawns*
- *Rosemary leaves*
- *Kosher salt& freshly ground black pepper*
- *3-4 cloves of minced garlic*

Instructions
In a bowl, mix all the ingredients and marinate the prawns in it for at least 60 minutes or more
Add two prawns and two slices of capsicum on each skewer.
Let the air fryer preheat to 356 C.
Cook for 5-6 minutes. Then change the temperature to 200 C and cook for another minute.
Serve with lemon wedges.

Nutritional value: Cal 194, Protein 26g, Carbs 12g, Fat 10g

Air-Fried Crumbed Fish

Prep Time: 10 mins

Cook Time: 12 mins

Servings: 2

Ingredients:

- *Four fish fillets*
- *Olive oil: 4 tablespoons*
- *One egg beaten*
- *Whole wheat breadcrumbs: ¼ cup*

Instructions:

Let the air fryer preheat to 356 ° F.

In a bowl, mix breadcrumbs with oil. Mix well

First, coat the fish in the egg mix (egg mix with water) then in the breadcrumb mix. Coat well

Place in the air fryer, let it cook for 10-12 minutes.

Serve hot with salad green and lemon.

Nutrition: 254 Kcal, Protein 15.5 g, Carbs 10.2 g, Fat 12.7 g

Parmesan Garlic Crusted Salmon

Prep Time: 5 mins

Cook Time: 15 mins

Servings: 2

Ingredients:

- *Whole wheat breadcrumbs: 1/4 cup*
- *4 cups of salmon*
- *Butter melted: 2 tablespoons*
    - *¼ tsp of freshly ground black pepper*
    - *Parmesan cheese: 1/4 cup(grated)*

- ◦ *Minced garlic: 2 teaspoons*
- ◦ *Half teaspoon of Italian seasoning*

Instructions:

Let the air fryer preheat to 400 F, spray the oil over the air fryer basket.

Pat dry the salmon. In a bowl, mix Parmesan cheese, Italian seasoning, and breadcrumbs. In another pan, mix melted butter with garlic and add to the breadcrumbs mix. Mix well

Add kosher salt and freshly ground black pepper to salmon. On top of every salmon piece, add the crust mix and press gently.

Let the air fryer preheat to 400 F and add salmon to it. Cook until done to your liking.

Serve hot with vegetable side dishes.

Nutritional value: 330 Kcal, Protein 31 g, Carbs 11g, Fat 19 g

Air Fryer Salmon with Soy Glaze

Prep   **Time:**   **5 mins**

Cook Time: 8 mins

Servings: 4

Ingredients:

- • *Gluten-free soy sauce: 3 tbsp.*
- • *Sriracha hot sauce: 1 tbsp.*
- • *One clove of minced garlic*
- • *Salmon: 4 fillets, skinless*

Instructions:

In a ziploc bag, mix sriracha, garlic, and soy sauce with salmon.

Mix well and let it marinate for at least half an hour.

Let the air fryer preheat to 400F with oil spray the basket

Take fish out from the marinade, pat dry.

Put the salmon in the air fryer, cook for 7 to 8 minutes, or longer.

In the meantime, in a saucepan, add the marinade, let it simmer until reduced to half.

Add glaze over salmon and serve.

Nutrition: 292 Kcal, Protein 35 g, Carbs 12 g, Fat 11 g

Air Fried Cajun Salmon

Prep   **Time:**   **10 mins**

              Cook Time: 20 mins

Servings: 1

Ingredients:

- *Fresh salmon: 1 piece*
- *Cajun seasoning: 2 tbsp.*
- *Lemon juice.*

Instructions:

Let the air fryer preheat to 356 F.

Pat dry the salmon fillet. Rub lemon juice and Cajun seasoning over the fish fillet.

Place in the air fryer, cook for 7 minutes. Serve with salad greens and lime wedges.

Nutrition: 216 Kcal, Protein 19.2 g, Carbs 5.6 g, Fat 19 g

Air Fryer Shrimp Scampi

Prep   **Time:**   **5 mins**

              Cook Time: 10 mins

Servings: 2

Ingredients:

- *Raw Shrimp: 4 cups*
- *Lemon Juice: 1 tablespoon*
- *Chopped fresh basil*
- *Red Pepper Flakes: 2 teaspoons*
- *Butter: 2.5 tablespoons*
- *Chopped chives*
- *Chicken Stock: 2 tablespoons*
- *Minced Garlic: 1 tablespoon*

Instructions

Let the air fryer preheat with a metal pan to 330F

In the hot pan, add garlic, red pepper flakes, and half of the butter. Let it cook for two minutes.

Add the butter, shrimp, chicken stock, minced garlic, chives, lemon juice, basil to the pan. Let it cook for five minutes. Bathe the shrimp in melted butter.

Take out from the air fryer and let it rest for one minute.

Add fresh basil leaves and chives and serve.

Nutrition: 287 Kcal, Protein 18 g, Carbs 7.5 g, Fat 5.5 g

Sesame Seeds Fish Fillet

Prep   Time: 10 mins

Cook Time: 20 mins

Servings: 2

Ingredients:

- *Plain flour: 3 tablespoons*
- *One egg, beaten*
- *Five frozen fish fillets*

For Coating:

- *Oil: 2 tablespoons*
- *Sesame seeds: 1/2 cup*
- *Rosemary herbs*
- *5-6 biscuit's crumbs*
- *Kosher salt& pepper, to taste*

Instructions:

For two-minute sauté the sesame seeds in a pan, without oil. Brown them and set it aside.

In a plate, mix all coating ingredients

Place the aluminum foil on the air fryer basket and let it preheat at 392 F.

First, coat the fish in flour. Then in egg, then in the coating mix.

Place in the Air fryer. If fillets are frozen, cook for ten minutes, then turn the fillet and cook for another four minutes.

If not frozen, then cook for eight minutes and two minutes.

Nutrition: 250 Kcal, Protein 20 g, Carbs 12.4 g, Fat 8 g

Lemon Pepper Shrimp in Air Fryer

Prep   **Time:**   **5 mins**

           Cook Time: 10 mins

Servings: 2

Ingredients:

- *Raw shrimp: 1 and 1/2 cup peeled, deveined*
- *Olive oil: 1/2 tablespoon*
- *Garlic powder: ¼ tsp*
- *Lemon pepper: 1 tsp*
- *Paprika: ¼ tsp*
- *Juice of one lemon*

Instructions:

Let the air fryer preheat to 400 F

In a bowl, mix lemon pepper, olive oil, paprika, garlic powder, and lemon juice. Mix well. Add shrimps and coat well

Add shrimps in the air fryer, cook for 6/8 minutes and top with lemon slices and serve

Nutrition: 237 Kcal, Protein 36 g, Carbs 11 g, Fat 6 g

Lemon Garlic Shrimp in Air Fryer

Prep   Time: 5 mins

Cook Time: 10 mins

Servings: 2

Ingredients:

- *Olive oil: 1 Tbsp.*
- *Small shrimp: 4 cups, peeled, tails removed*

- *One lemon juice and zest*
- *Parsley: 1/4 cup sliced*
- *Red pepper flakes (crushed): 1 pinch*

- *Four cloves of grated garlic*
- *Sea salt: 1/4 teaspoon*

Instructions:

Let air fryer heat to 400F

Mix olive oil, lemon zest, red pepper flakes, shrimp, kosher salt, and garlic in a bowl and coat the shrimp well.

Place shrimps in the air fryer basket, coat with oil spray.

Cook at 400 F for 8 minutes. Toss the shrimp halfway through

Serve with lemon slices and parsley.

Nutrition: per serving: 140 kcal, Protein 20g, Net Carbs 8g, Fat: 18g

Air Fried Shrimp with Delicious Sauce

Prep   Time: 10 mins

Cook Time: 20 mins

Servings: 4

Ingredients:

- *Whole wheat bread crumbs: 3/4 cup*
- *Raw shrimp: 4 cups, deveined, peeled*
- *Flour: half cup*
- *Paprika: one tsp*
- *Chicken Seasoning, to taste*
- *2 tbsp. of one egg white*
- *Kosher salt and pepper to taste*

Sauce:

- *Sweet chili sauce: 1/4 cup*
- *Plain Greek yogurt: 1/3 cup*
- *Sriracha: 2 tbsp.*

Instructions:

Let the Air Fryer preheat to 400 degrees.

Add the seasonings to shrimp and coat well.

In three separate bowls, add flour, bread crumbs, and egg whites.

First coat the shrimp in flour, dab lightly in egg whites, then in the bread crumbs.

With cooking oil, spray the shrimp.

Place the shrimps in an air fryer, cook for four minutes, turn the shrimp over, and cook for another four minutes. Serve with micro green and sauce.

Sauce:
In a small bowl, mix all the ingredients. And serve.

Nutrition: 229 kcal, Protein 22g, Carbs 13g, Fat 10g

Air Fryer Crab Cakes

Prep **Time:** **10 mins**

Cook Time: 20 mins

Servings: 6

Ingredients:

- *Crab meat: 4 cups*
- *Two eggs*
- *Whole wheat bread crumbs: ¼ cup*
- *Mayonnaise: 2 tablespoons*
- *Worcestershire sauce: 1 teaspoon*
- *Old Bay seasoning: 1 and ½ teaspoon*
- *Dijon mustard: 1 teaspoon*
- *Freshly ground black pepper to taste*
- *Green onion: ¼ cup, chopped*

Instructions:
In a bowl, add Dijon mustard, Old Bay, eggs, Worcestershire, and mayonnaise mix it well. Then add in the chopped green onion and mix.

Fold in the crab meat to mayonnaise mix. Then add breadcrumbs, not to over mix.

Chill the mix in the refrigerator for at least 60 minutes. Then shape into patties.

Let the air-fryer preheat to 350F. Cook for 10 minutes. Flip the patties halfway through.

Serve with lemon wedges.

Nutrition: 218 kcal, Protein 16.7g Carbs 5.6 g, Fat 13 g

Air Fryer Tuna Patties

Prep   **Time:**   **15 mins**
          Cook Time: 10 mins
Servings: 10

Ingredients:

- *Whole wheat breadcrumbs: half cup*
- *Fresh tuna: 4 cups, diced*
- *Lemon zest*
- *Lemon juice: 1 Tablespoon*
- *1 egg*
- *Grated parmesan cheese: 3 Tablespoons*
- *One chopped stalk celery*
- *Garlic powder: half teaspoon*
- *Dried herbs: half teaspoon*
- *Minced onion: 3 Tablespoons*
- *Salt to taste*
- *Freshly ground black pepper*

Instructions:

In a bowl, add lemon zest, bread crumbs, salt, pepper, celery, eggs, dried herbs, lemon juice, garlic powder, parmesan cheese, and onion. Mix everything. Then add in tuna gently. Shape into patties. If the mixture is too loose, cool in the refrigerator.

Add air fryer baking paper in the air fryer basket. Spray the baking paper with cooking spray.

Spray the patties with oil.

Cook for ten minutes at 360°F. turn the patties halfway over.

Serve with lemon slices.

Nutrition: 214 kcal, Protein 22g, Carbs 6g, Fat 15g

Fish Finger Sandwich

Prep   **Time:**   **10 mins**

Cook Time: 20 mins

Servings: 3

Ingredients:

- *Greek yogurt: 1 tbsp.*
- *Cod fillets: 4, without skin*
- *Flour: 2 tbsp.*
- *Whole-wheat breadcrumbs: 5 tbsp.*
- *Kosher salt and pepper to taste*
- *Capers: 10–12*
- *Frozen peas: 3/4 cup*
- *Lemon juice*

Instructions:

Let the air fryer preheat.

Sprinkle kosher salt and pepper on the cod fillets, and coat in flour, then in breadcrumbs

Spray the fryer basket with oil. Put the cod fillets in the basket.

Cook for 15 minutes at 200 C.

In the meantime, cook the peas in boiling water for a few minutes. Take out from the water and blend with Greek yogurt, lemon juice, and capers until well combined.

On a bun, add cooked fish with pea puree. Add lettuce and tomato.

Nutrition: 240 kcal, Protein 20g, Carbs 7g, Fat 12g

Lime-Garlic Shrimp Kebabs

Prep   **Time:**   **5 mins**

Servings: 2

Ingredients:

- *One lime*
- *Raw shrimp: 1 cup*
- *Salt: 1/8 teaspoon*
- *1 clove of garlic*
- *Freshly ground black pepper*

Instructions:

In water, let wooden skewers soak for 20 minutes.

Let the Air fryer preheat to 350F.

In a bowl, mix shrimp, minced garlic, lime juice, kosher salt, and pepper

Add shrimp on skewers.

Place skewers in the air fryer, and cook for 8 minutes. Turn halfway over.

Top with cilantro and serve with your favorite dip.

Nutrition: 76 kcal, Protein 13g, Carbs 4g, Fat 9 g

Air Fryer Sushi Roll

Prep Time: 1 hour 30 minutes
Cook Time: 10 mins
Servings: 3

Ingredients:
For the Kale Salad:

- *Rice vinegar: half teaspoon*
- *Chopped kale: one and a 1/2 cups*
- *Garlic powder:1/8 teaspoon*
- *Sesame seeds: 1 tablespoon*

- *Toasted sesame oil: 3/4 teaspoon*
- *Ground ginger: 1/4 teaspoon*
- *Soy sauce: 3/4 teaspoon*
- *Sushi Rolls*
- *Half avocado - sliced*
- *Cooked Sushi Rice - cooled*
- *Whole wheat breadcrumbs: half cup*
- *Sushi: 3 sheets*

Instructions:

Kale Salad:

In a bowl, add vinegar, garlic powder, kale, soy sauce, sesame oil, and ground ginger. With your hands, mix with sesame seeds and set it aside.

Sushi Rolls

Lay a sheet of sushi on a flat surface. With damp fingertips, add a tablespoon of rice, and spread it on the sheet. Cover the sheet with rice, leaving a half-inch space at one end.

Add kale salad with avocado slices. Roll up the sushi, use water if needed.

Add the breadcrumbs in a bowl. Coat the sushi roll with Sriracha Mayo, then in breadcrumbs.

Add the rolls to the air fryer. Cook for ten minutes at 390 F, shake the basket halfway through.

Take out from the fryer, and let them cool, then cut with a sharp knife.

Serve with light soy sauce.

Nutrition: 369 kcal, Protein 26.3 g, Carbs 15g, Fat 13.9g

Roasted Salmon with Fennel Salad

Prep   **Time:**   **15**
minutes   **Cook**
Time: 10 mins
Servings: 4

Ingredients:

- *Skinless and center-cut: 4 salmon fillets*
- *Lemon juice: 1 teaspoon (fresh)*
- *Parsley: 2 teaspoons (chopped)*
- *Salt: 1 teaspoon, divided*
- *Olive oil: 2 tablespoons*
- *Chopped thyme: 1 teaspoon*
- *Fennel heads: 4 cups (thinly sliced)*
- *One clove of minced garlic*
- *Fresh dill: 2 tablespoons, chopped*
- *Greek yogurt: 2/3 cup (reduced-fat)*

Instructions:

In a bowl, add half teaspoon of salt, parsley, and thyme, mix well. Rub oil over salmon, and sprinkle with thyme mixture.

Put salmon fillets in the air fryer basket, cook for ten minutes at 350°F.

In the meantime, mix garlic, fennel, yogurt, half tsp. of salt, dill, lemon juice in a bowl.

Serve with fennel salad.

Nutrition: 364kcal, Protein 38g, Carbs 9g, Fat 30g

Catfish with Green Beans, in Southern Style

Prep   **Time:**   **10**
minutes   **Cook**
Time: 20 mins
Servings: 2

Ingredients:

- *Catfish fillets: 2 pieces*
- *Green beans: half cup, trimmed*
- *Freshly ground black pepper and salt, to taste divided*
- *Crushed red pepper: half tsp.*
- *Flour: 1/4 cup*
- *One egg, lightly beaten*
- *Dill pickle relish: 3/4 teaspoon*
- *Apple cider vinegar: half tsp*
- *1/3 cup whole-wheat breadcrumbs*
- *Mayonnaise: 2 tablespoons*
- *Dill*
- *Lemon wedges*

Instructions:

In a bowl, add green beans, spray them with cooking oil. Coat with crushed red pepper, 1/8 teaspoon of kosher salt, and half tsp. Of honey and cook in the air fryer at 400 F until soft and browned, for 12 minutes. Take out from fryer and cover with aluminum foil
In the meantime, coat catfish in flour. Then dip in egg to coat, then in breadcrumbs. Place fish in an air fryer basket and spray with cooking oil.
Cook for 8 minutes, at 400ºF, until cooked through and golden brown.
Sprinkle with pepper and salt. In the meantime, mix vinegar, dill, relish, mayonnaise, in a bowl. Serve the sauce with fish and green beans.

Nutrition: 243 kcal, Protein 33 g, Carbs 18 g, Fat 18 g

Sriracha Tossed Calamari

Prep   **Time:**   **10**
minutes   **Cook**
Time: 20 mins

Servings: 2

Ingredients:

- *Club soda: 1 cup*
- *Sriracha: 1-2 Tbsp.*
- *Calamari tubes: 2 cups*
- *Flour: 1 cup*
- *Pinches of salt, freshly ground black pepper, red pepper flakes, and red pepper*

Instructions:

Cut the calamari tubes into rings. Submerge them with club soda. Let it rest for ten minutes.

In the meantime, in a bowl, add freshly ground black pepper, flour, red pepper, and kosher salt and mix well.

Drain the calamari and pat dry with a paper towel. Coat well the calamari in the flour mix and set aside.

Spray oil in the air fryer basket and put calamari in one single layer. Cook at 375 ° F for 11 minutes. Toss the rings twice while cooking. Meanwhile, to make sauce, add red pepper flakes, and sriracha in a bowl, mix well.

Take calamari out from the basket, mix with sauce cook for another two minutes more. Serve with salad green.

Nutrition: 252 kcal, Protein 41 g, Carbs 3.1 g, Fat: 38 g

Scallops with Creamy Tomato Sauce

Prep   **Time:**   **5**
minutes   **Cook**
Time: 10 mins
Servings: 2

Ingredients:

- *Sea scallops eight jumbo*

- *Tomato Paste: 1 tbsp.*
- *Chopped fresh basil one tablespoon*

- *3/4 cup of low-fat Whipping Cream*
- *Kosher salt half teaspoon*
- *Ground Freshly black pepper half teaspoon*

- *Minced garlic 1 teaspoon*
- *Frozen Spinach, thawed half cup*
- *Oil Spray*

Instructions:

Take a seven-inch pan (heatproof) and add spinach in a single layer at the bottom

Rub olive oil on both sides of scallops, season with kosher salt and pepper.

On top of the spinach, place the seasoned scallops

Put the pan in the air fryer and cook for ten minutes at 350F, until scallops are cooked completely, and internal temperature reaches 135F.

Serve immediately.

Nutrition: 259kcal, Protein 19g, Carbs 6g, Fat 13g

Shrimp Spring Rolls in Air Fryer

Prep   **Time:**   **10**
minutes   **Cook**
Time: 25 mins
Servings: 4

Ingredients:

- *Deveined raw shrimp: half cup chopped (peeled)*
- *Olive oil: 2 and 1/2 tbsp.*
- *Matchstick carrots: 1 cup*

- *Slices of red bell pepper: 1 cup*
- *Red pepper: 1/4 teaspoon (crushed)*
- *Slices of snow peas: 3/4 cup*
- *Shredded cabbage: 2 cups*
- *Lime juice: 1 tablespoon*
- *Sweet chili sauce: half cup*
- *Fish sauce: 2 teaspoons*
- *Eight spring roll (wrappers)*

Instructions:

In a skillet, add one and a half tbsp. of olive, until smoking lightly. Stir in bell pepper, cabbage, carrots, and cook for two minutes. Turn off the heat, take out in a dish and cool for five minutes.

In a bowl, add shrimp, lime juice, cabbage mixture, crushed red pepper, fish sauce, and snow peas. Mix well

Lay spring roll wrappers on a plate. Add 1/4 cup of filling in the middle of each wrapper. Fold tightly with water. Brush the olive oil over folded rolls.

Put spring rolls in the air fryer basket and cook for 6 to 7 minutes at 390°F until light brown and crispy.

You may serve with sweet chili sauce.

Nutrition: 180 kcal, Protein 17 g, Carbs 9 g, Fat 9 g

VEGETABLES

Vegetable Stock for Diabetics

Prep   **Time:**   **5 mins**

Cook Time: 3 hours

Servings: 7 U.S. pints

Ingredients:

- *Two onions*
- *Two leeks*
- *Three celery ribs*
- *Two carrots*
- *One chopped parsnip*
- *One-pound peeled celery root*
- *Half cup shallot*
- *Three and a half quarts water*
- *One cup fresh parsley (stems and leaves)*
- *Two bay leaves*
- *Two tablespoons black peppercorns*

Instructions

Combine the vegetables and water in a crockpot. Bring to a simmer. Add parsley, bay leaves, and peppercorns.

Cook for around 3 hours on low and check it regularly, adding more water if required, to hold ingredients covered.

Strain the vegetables through a fine sieve.

Nutrition: 80.8 Kcal, Protein 2.5 g, Carbs 17.7 g, Fat 0.4 g, Sugars 4 g

Mushroom Soup

Prep Time: 10 Minutes   **Cook**
Time: 20 minutes
Servings: 2

Ingredients:

- *1 cup Cremini mushrooms, chopped*
- *1 cup Cheddar cheese, shredded*
- *2 cups of water*
- *½ teaspoon salt*
- *1 teaspoon dried thyme*
- *½ teaspoon dried oregano*
- *1 tablespoon fresh parsley, chopped*
- *1 tablespoon olive oil*
- *1 bell pepper, chopped*

Instructions:

Pour olive oil in the pan. Add mushrooms and bell pepper. Roast the vegetables for 5 minutes over the medium heat. Then sprinkle them with salt, thyme, and dried oregano. Add parsley and water. Stir the soup well. Cook the soup for 10 minutes.

After this, blend the soup until it is smooth and simmer it for 5 minutes more. Add cheese and stir until cheese is melted.

Ladle the cooked soup into the bowls.

Nutrition: Calories 320, Fat 26 g, Carbs 7.4 g, Protein 15.7 g

Vegetarian Spinach Rolls

Prep   **Time:**   **10**
mins
                Cook Time: 40 mins
Servings: 2

Ingredients:

- *Sixteen ounces frozen spinach leaves*

- *Three eggs*
- *Two and a half lb. onion*
- *Two ounces carrot*
- *One-ounce low-fat mozzarella cheese*
- *Four ounces fat-free cottage cheese*
- *Three quarter cup parsley*
- *One cloves garlic*
- *One tablespoon curry powder*
- *One fourth tablespoon chili flakes*
- *One tablespoon salt*
- *One tablespoon pepper*
- *Cooking spray*

Instructions

Preheat the oven to 400 ° F.

Thaw the spinach and drain the water with a strainer.

In a mixing bowl, mix the spinach, 2 eggs, mozzarella, garlic, half the salt, and pepper.

Spray a baking sheet with cooking spray. Move the spinach mixture to the sheet and push it down, approximately half an inch thick and about 10 to 12 inches in height. Bake for 15 minutes and then set aside on a rack to cool. Don't turn the oven off.

Chop the onion and parsley finely. Grate the carrots. Fry the onions for about a minute in a skillet with a little oil. Then add to the pan the carrots and parsley and let it boil for around 2 min.

Add cottage cheese, curry, chili, the other half of the salt, and pepper. Briefly mix.

Take the fire off the pan, put an egg, and blend it all together.

Spread the filling over the spinach that has been cooled.

Roll the spinach mat carefully, then bake for 25 minutes.

Take out the roll once the time is up and let it cool for 5-10 minutes before cutting it into slices and serving.

Nutrition: 308 Kcal, Protein 26.2 g, Carbs 18.9 g, Fat 9.7 g, Sugars 5.6 g

Vegetable Chili

Prep   Time: 15 mins
              Cook Time: 1 hour
Servings: 4

Ingredients:

- *Two finely chopped onions*
- *One finely chopped red pepper*
- *One and a half cups finely chopped carrots*
- *One courgette, finely chopped*
- *1 cup finely chopped mushrooms,*
- *One tablespoon chili powder*
- *One tablespoon ground cumin*
- *One tablespoon oregano*
- *Eight and a half cups tin chopped tomatoes*
- *14 oz. canned lentils*
- *14 oz. tin mixed beans in water*
- *One tablespoon tomato ketchup*
- *Two tablespoons sugar*
- *One tablespoon salt*

Instructions

In a wide skillet, heat the oil, add the onions, and cook for 5–8 minutes before they begin to brown. Add the red pepper, onions, zucchini, and mushrooms and cook for another 10 minutes.
Then add chili powder, cumin, oregano, and tomatoes. Mix together, then simmer for an additional 10 minutes.
Add water, ketchup, sugar, and salt, lentils and beans. Mix thoroughly, apply the lid and get to a soft bubble for 30 minutes.

Nutrition: 127 Kcal, Protein 8.3 g, Carbs 17.2 g, Fat 1 g, Sugars 8 g

Vegetarian Hot and Sour Soup

Prep   **Time:**   **15 mins**

Cook Time: 1 hour

Servings: 4

Ingredients:

- *Four dried Chinese black mushrooms*
- *Hot water*
- *Two tablespoons canola oil*
- *One carrot, peeled and julienned*
- *Five cups vegetable broth*
- *A quarter cup canned bamboo shoots*
- *Three tablespoons cornstarch, dissolved in quarter cup cold water*
- *Three tablespoons low-sodium soy sauce*
- *One-third cup rice vinegar*
- *Three-quarter tablespoon ground white pepper*
- *Six ounces savory firm tofu, julienned*
- *Two lightly beaten eggs*
- *Two thinly sliced green onion*

Instructions

In a shallow bowl, soak the dried mushrooms in hot water for 20 minutes or until softened. Cut into slim slices, and discard the roots and other rough places.

Heat canola oil over medium-high heat in a stock pot. Add the carrots and mushrooms and cook for 2 minutes. Add the bamboo shoots and broth and get it to a boil. Apply the cornstarch mixture and stir for around 2 minutes before the soup thickens. Add soy sauce, white pepper, onions, and rice vinegar.

Add the tofu and get the broth to a boil again. Pour eggs into soup, and continue mixing in the same direction.

Serve immediately.

Nutrition: 81 Kcal, Protein 3.9 g, Carbs 8.7 g, Fat 3.7 g

Swiss Chard with Raisins & Pine Nuts

Prep   **Time:**   **15 mins**

                Cook Time: 20 mins

Servings: 4

Ingredients:

- *Two pounds Swiss chard, stemmed (the stems diced)*
- *Vegetable broth*
- *Two minced garlic cloves*
- *Three tablespoons of raisins*

- *Three tablespoons of pine nuts*
- *Salt and ground black pepper*

Instructions

Put the raisins in a bowl and cover them with hot water. Soak for 10 minutes and rinse.

Fill a cup of ice water.

Over low heat, place a large pot of water on the stove and incorporate the chard. Cook for 2-3 minutes. Then move the chard to the ice water bowl and leave to rest for a minute. As much water as practicable, rinse and strain out and coarsely chop.

In a large pan, boil ½ cup of vegetable broth. Add the chard stems and cook until soft, about 3 to 5 minutes. Add the pine nuts and cook for another minute, stirring. Add the garlic and simmer for an extra minute or two. If it sticks, add more vegetable broth.

Mix together the sliced vegetables and raisins. With a little salt and ground black pepper, season to taste, and eat.

Nutrition: 151 Kcal, Protein 4.8 g, Carbs 15.2 g, Fat 10.1 g

Cucumber Chunks with Avocado

Prep Time: 10 minutes

Servings: 5

Ingredients:

- *1 cucumber*
- *5 cherry tomatoes*
- *2 oz. avocado, pitted*
- *¼ tsp. minced garlic*
- *¼ tsp. dried basil*
- *¾ tsp. lemon juice*

Instructions

Trim the cucumber and slice it on 5 thick slices.

After this, churn avocado until you get cream mass.

Add minced garlic, dried basil, and lemon juice. Mix up well.

Spread the avocado mass over the cucumber slices and top it with cherry tomatoes.

Nutrition: 56 Kcal, Fat: 2.7 g, Carbs: 8.1 g, Protein: 1.9 g

Cucumber Tomato Okra Salsa

Prep Time: 10 minutes

Cook Time: 15 minutes

Servings: 4

Ingredients:

- *1 lb. tomatoes, chopped*
- *1/4 tsp. red pepper flakes*
- *1/4 cup fresh lemon juice*
- *1 cucumber, chopped*
- *1 tbsp. oregano, chopped*
- *1 tbsp. fresh basil, chopped*

- *1 tbsp. olive oil*
- *1 onion, chopped*
- *1 tbsp. garlic, chopped*
- *1 1/2 cups okra, chopped*
- *Salt and pepper*

Instructions

Add oil into the inner pot of instant pot and set the pot on sauté mode.

Add onion, garlic, pepper, and salt and sauté for 3 minutes. Add remaining ingredients except for cucumber and stir well. Seal pot with lid and cook on high for 12 minutes.

Allow to release pressure for 10 minutes then release remaining using quick release. Remove lid.

Then add cucumber and mix well.

Nutrition: 97 Kcal, Fat 4.1 g, Carbs 13 g, Protein 2.8 g

Lemon Cauliflower Florets

Prep Time: 15 minutes
> **Cook Time: 15 minutes**

Servings: 6

Ingredients:

- *1-pound cauliflower head, trimmed*
- *3 tbsps. lemon juice*
- *3 eggs, beaten*
- *1 tsp. salt*
- *1 tsp. ground black pepper*
- *2 cups water, for cooking*
- *3 tbsps. Olive oil*
- *1 tsp. turmeric*

Instructions

Place the cauliflower head in the pan. Add water and boil the cauliflower for 8 minutes. Then cool the vegetable well and separate it onto the florets.

Whisk together eggs, salt, ground black pepper, and turmeric.

Dip every cauliflower floret in the egg mixture.

Toss the olive oil in the skillet and heat it up. Roast the cauliflower florets for 2 minutes from each side over the medium heat.

Sprinkle the cooked florets with lemon juice.

Nutrition: 101 Kcal, Fat: 6.6 g, Carbs: 6.1 g, Protein: 5.9 g

SALADS

Diced Vegetable Salad

Prep Time: 15 minutes

Servings: 8

Ingredients:

- Two diced small zucchinis
- Half cucumber, diced
- One diced red bell pepper
- One diced green bell pepper
- One diced yellow bell pepper
- Half diced red onion
- One diced hot house tomato
- One cup of cooked chickpeas
- Half cup roughly chopped parsley
- One cup crumbled feta cheese

For dressing:

- One minced clove garlic
- Half tablespoon kosher salt
- One tablespoon freshly ground black pepper
- One tablespoon dried oregano
- Half cup olive oil
- Three tablespoons red wine vinegar

Instructions

Mix all vegetables in a big bowl with the cheese.
In another bowl, whisk the remaining ingredients together to create the dressing.
Pour the salad over the dressing and blend softly to absorb it.

Nutrition: Calories 61, Fat 3.4 g, Carbohydrates 8 g, Protein 0.9 g,
Sugars 3 g

Diabetic Chicken Salad

**Prep Time: 5
minutes**

Cook Time: 25 mins Servings: 6

Ingredients:

For chicken:

- *Two pounds boneless chicken thighs*
- *Olive oil spray*
- *Half tablespoon pepper*
- *Half tablespoon garlic powder*
- *Half tablespoon onion powder*
- *Half tablespoon salt*

For salad:

- *Three cups kale, chopped into slices*
- *One cup Brussel sprouts, chopped into slices*
- *One cup purple cabbage, sliced*
- *One carrot, sliced thinly*
- *One thinly sliced red onion*
- *One thinly sliced small stalk of fennel*
- *One cucumber, chopped into bite-sized pieces*
- *One-quarter cup pomegranate seeds*
- *One diced tomato*
- *A quarter cup crumbled feta*

For Vinaigrette:

- *A quarter cup extra virgin olive oil*
- *One and a half lemons' juice*
- *One tablespoon minced fennel*
- *Salt and pepper to taste*

Instructions

Preheat the oven to 375°F. Spray a small pan with olive oil and spread the seasonings on the chicken thighs on both sides.

Put in a skillet and cook for 30 minutes or until the thickest section of the thigh is 165°F. Enable to cool and put aside.

Prepare the salad ingredients when the chicken is cooking. Chop the cabbage, the sprouts, cucumber, purple cabbage, red onion, and fennel. Cut the tomato into dices. Mix the ingredients in a big bowl, then put them in the fridge.

Combine all the vinaigrette ingredients and mix well. Put in the fridge until necessary.

Chop the chicken into bite-sized bits, and put over the salad. Drizzle and toss in the vinaigrette.

Nutrition: Calories 321, Fat 16.2 g, Carbohydrates 13.7 g, Protein 30.4 g, Sugars 5 g

Waldorf Salad

Prep Time: 15 minutes

Servings: 4

Ingredients:

- *One tablespoon lemon juice*
- *Two and a half cups diced apples*
- *One cup celery*
- *Half cup walnuts*
- *One dash salt*
- *Half cup low-fat yogurt*
- *Two tablespoons low-fat mayonnaise*

Instructions

Drizzle diced apples with lemon juice; toss properly.

Add in the walnuts and celery.
Blend salt, low-fat yogurt, and mayonnaise together.
Add into the combination of apples.

Nutrition: Calories 165, Fat 9 g, Carbohydrates 17 g, Protein 4 g, Sugars 8.9 g

Beans Salad

Prep Time: 5 minutes

Servings: 4

Ingredients:

- *Three cups mixed boiled beans*
- *Half cup onions, sliced*
- *Three quarter cup Tomatoes, diced*
- *One tablespoon Oil*
- *Two tablespoons Lemon juice*
- *One tablespoon Basil, chopped*
- *Half tablespoon Garlic, chopped*
- *Salt and pepper*
- *Two tablespoons Coriander, chopped*

Instructions

Mix all the ingredients together thoroughly. Sprinkle with chopped coriander and serve.

Nutrition: Calories 51, Fat 0 g, Carbohydrates 10 g, Protein 1.9 g

Sweet Potato, Carrot and Asparagus Salad

Prep Time: 10 minutes

Cook Time: 20 mins Servings: 6

Ingredients:

- *Two sweet potatoes, peeled and sliced into large chunks*
- *One carrot, peeled and sliced into large chunks*
- *One and half cups asparagus, trimmed*
- *1/2 cup broad beans*
- *1/2 cup frozen peas*

For dressing:

- *Eight to ten finely chopped cornichons*
- *Two tablespoons Greek-style yogurt*
- *One tablespoon low fat mayonnaise*
- *One tsp Dijon mustard*
- *A pinch of pepper*

Instructions

In a pot of boiling water, add the potatoes and carrots and cook for 10 minutes. Add the asparagus and continue boiling for 5 minutes. Turn off the heat after the vegetables are cooked, and transfer the fava beans and peas. This will thaw them but avoid overcooking the other vegetables.

Drain the vegetables, and let them cool.

Create the dressing by adding all the ingredients.

Add the dressing to the vegetables and serve.

Nutrition: Calories 111, Fat 1.3 g, Carbohydrates 18 g, Protein 3.4 g, Sugars 6.7 g

DESSERTS

Cherry and Chocolate Dessert

Prep Time: 15 minutes

Cook Time: 15 mins Servings: 4

Ingredients:

- *Two cups fresh cherries*
- *Two tablespoons artificial sweetener*
- *One tablespoon level corn flour, blended with one tablespoon cold water*
- *Low-fat soft cheese*
- *Two tablespoons skimmed milk*
- *half level tsp vanilla extract*

For the chocolate sauce:

- 1/4 cup dark chocolate, broken into pieces
- One tablespoon unsweetened cocoa powder
- Half tablespoon corn flour, blended with half tbsp cold water
- One tablespoon golden syrup

Instructions

Halve the cherries and pit them, reserving 4 entire ones for decoration.

Put 4 tbsp of water and 1 tbsp of the sweetener in a small pot. Simmer until soft for 3-4 minutes.

Mix in the corn flour and cold water and stir in the cherries. Remove from the heat, stirring to prevent the skin from forming.

In a bowl, combine the cheese, skim milk, vanilla extract, and remaining sweetener. Mix well until smooth.

In another bowl, place the dark chocolate chunks, cocoa powder, cornmeal (along with cold water), and golden syrup, to make the chocolate sauce. Heat everything in a small saucepan, stirring constantly, until smooth. Allow to cool, continuing to stir.

Add everything into small glasses. Serve each one with a cherry.

Nutrition: Calories 114, Fat 2 g, Carbohydrates 17 g, Protein 5 g, Sugars 14 g

Carrot Cake

Prep Time: 10 minutes

Cook Time: 25 mins Servings: 14

Ingredients:

- *Half cup flour*
- *Two-third cup flax seed meal*
- *Two tablespoons baking powder*

- *One tablespoon pumpkin pie spices*
- *Half tablespoon baking soda*
- *A quarter tablespoon salt*
- *Three cups finely shredded carrot*
- *4 eggs*
- *Half cup sugar substitute blend*
- *Half cup brown sugar substitute blend*
- *Half cup canola oil*

Instructions

Preheat the oven to 350 ° F. Grease a baking sheet and apply a waxed paper to the bottom. Grease the waxed paper and the sides of the pan and lightly flour it.

Stir the flour, flaxseed meal, baking powder, pumpkin pie spices, baking soda, and salt together in a wide bowl; set aside.

Combine the carrot, eggs, sugar substitute, brown sugar substitute, and oil in another large bowl.

Combine the egg mixture to the flour mixture and stir.

Spoon all into the prepared pan, uniformly spreading.

Bake for 25 to 30 minutes. Cool for 10 minutes and serve.

Nutrition: Calories 206, Fat 9 g, Carbohydrates 24 g, Protein 3.8 g, Sugars 11 g

Low-Carb, Sugar Free Peanut Butter Cookies

Prep Time: 5 minutes

Cook Time: 15 mins Servings: 12

One Cookie per serving

Ingredients:

- *One cup smooth peanut butter with no sugar*
- *One egg*

- *Two-third cup erythritol*
- *Half tablespoon baking soda*
- *Half tablespoon vanilla essence*

Instructions

Preheat oven to 350°F and place a sheet of baking paper on a cookie sheet.

In a blender, add the erythritol and mix until it turns to a powder.

In a medium mixing bowl, incorporate all ingredients and combine until a thick, glossy dough develops.

Form a ball with the dough, then flattened balls of about 2 tablespoons of dough. Place them on the prepared baking sheet.

Bake the cookies for 12 to 15 minutes.

Remove from oven and let cool for about 25 minutes before serving.

Nutrition: Calories 139, Fat 9.5 g, Carbohydrates 4.1 g, Protein 5.3 g, Sugars 0 g

Apple Cheesecake

Prep Time: 5 minutes

Cook Time: 15 mins Servings: 12

Ingredients:

For crust:

- *Half cup graham cracker crumbs*
- *A quarter cup butter, melted*
- *2 tablespoons Equal sweetener*

For Cheesecake:

- *16 oz reduced-fat cream cheese, softened*
- *1 cup Equal sweetener*
- *3 cups unsweetened applesauce*

- *2 whole eggs*
- *2 egg whites*
- *2 tablespoons lemon juice*
- *Two tablespoons cornstarch*
- *Three fourth tablespoon ground cinnamon*
- *Half tsp apple pie spice*
- *One tablespoon vanilla extract*
- *One cup reduced-fat sour cream*

Instructions

Preheat the oven to 325°F

Blend all ingredients for the crust.

Press the mixture to the bottom of a baking pan. 10 minutes to bake. Cool while baking the cheesecake.

Beat the cream cheese and sweetener in a medium-speed mixing bowl until smooth and well mixed.

Add applesauce, eggs, egg whites, and lemon juice, and stir. Add the cornstarch, apple pie seasoning, cinnamon, and vanilla, and continue to stir. Fold in sour cream and combining.

Pour the combination of cheesecake over the cooked crust.

Bake for 45 to 50 minutes.

Let the cheesecake absolutely cool off before cover and refrigerate for several hours.

Nutrition: Calories 197, Fat 12 g, Carbohydrates 14 g, Protein 5.9 g

Peach-Berry Frozen Dessert

Prep Time: 10 minutes

Servings: 9

Ingredients:

- *Eight oz fat-free cream cheese*
- *Six oz fat-free yogurt with artificial sweetener*

- *Twelve oz frozen light whipped dessert topping, thawed*
- *One cup chopped, peeled fresh peaches*
- *One cup frozen unsweetened blueberries, raspberries*
- *One sprig Fresh mint leaves*
- *Berries to garnish*

Instructions

Combine the cream cheese and yogurt in a bowl. Beat until smooth. Fold in the whipped topping, the 1 cup of berries, and the peaches. Pour into a baking dish. Cover and freeze for around 8 hours.

To serve, leave to thaw slightly at room temperature for around 45 minutes. Garnish with mint leaves and berries.

Nutrition: Calories 88, Fat 1.7 g, Carbohydrates 11.5 g, Protein 5.3 g, Sugars 3 g

Simple Coconut Porridge

Prep Time: 15 minutes   **Servings: 6**

Ingredients:

- *Powdered erythritol as needed*
- *1 ½ cups almond milk, unsweetened*
- *2 tablespoons protein powder*
- *3 tablespoons Golden Flaxseed meal*
- *2 tablespoons coconut flour*

Instructions:

Take a bowl and mix in flaxseed meal, protein powder, coconut flour and mix well.

Add mix to saucepan (placed over medium heat).

Add almond milk and stir, let the mixture thicken.

Add your desired amount of sweetener and serve.

Nutrition: Calories: 259 g Fat: 13 g Carbs: 5 g Protein: 16 g

AIR FRY RECIPES

Air Fried Chocolate Soufflé

Prep Time: 15 minutes **Cook time: 15 minutes**
Servings: 2

Ingredients:

- *Milk: 1/3 cup*
- *Butter soft to melted: 2 tbsp.*
- *Flour: 1 tbsp.*
- *Splenda: 2 tbsp.*
- *One Egg Yolk*
- *Sugar-Free Chocolate Chips: 1/4 cup*
- *Two egg whites*
- *Half teaspoon of cream of tartare*
- *Half teaspoon of Vanilla Extract*

Instructions:
Grease the ramekins with spray oil or softened butter.
Sprinkle with any sugar alternative, make sure to cover them.
Let the air fryer preheat to 325-330 F.
Melt the chocolate in a microwave-safe bowl. Mix every 30 seconds until fully melted.
Or use a double boiler method.
Melt the one and a half tablespoons of butter over low-medium heat. In a small-sized skillet.
Once the butter has melted, then whisk in the flour. Keep whisking until thickened. Then turn the heat off.

Add the egg whites with cream of tartar, with the whisk attachment, in a stand mixer, mix until peaks forms.

Meanwhile, combine the ingredients in a melted chocolate bowl, add the flour mixture and melted butter to chocolate, and blend. Add in the vanilla extract, egg yolks, remaining sugar alternative.

Fold the egg white peaks gently with the ingredients into the bowl.

Add the mix into ramekins about 3/4 full of five-ounce ramekins.

Let it bake for 12-14 minutes, or until done.

Nutrition: 288 kcal, Protein 6 g, Carbs 5 g, Fat 24 g

Sugar-Free Carrot Cake

Prep Time: 15 minutes   **Cook time: 40 minutes**
Servings: 8

Ingredients:

- *All-Purpose Flour: 1 ¼ cups*
- *Pumpkin Pie Spice: 1 tsp*
- *Baking Powder: one teaspoon*
- *Splenda: 3/4 cup*
- *Carrots: 2 cups–grated*
- *2 Eggs*
- *Baking Soda: half teaspoon*
- *Canola Oil: ¾ cup*

Instructions

Let the air fryer preheat to 350 F. spray the cake pan with oil spray, and add a pinch of flour over that.

In a bowl, combine the baking powder, flour, pumpkin pie spice, and baking soda.

In another bowl, mix the eggs, oil, and sugar alternative. Now combine the dry to wet ingredients. Add in the grated carrots.
Add the cake batter to the greased cake pan.
Place the cake pan in the basket of the air fryer. Let it Air fry for half an hour, but do not let the top too brown.
Air fry for 35-40 minutes in total.

Nutrition: Calories 286, Fat 21 g, Carbohydrates 18 g, Protein 4 g

Sugar-Free Cheesecake

Prep Time: 20 minutes

Cook time:

30 minutes
Servings: 18

Ingredients:

- *Splenda: half cup*
- *One and a half Cream Cheese*
- *Two Eggs*
- *Vanilla Extract: 1 tsp*

Instructions
Let the oven preheat to 300 F.
Spray the muffin pan with oil.
In a bowl, add the sugar alternative, vanilla extract, and cream cheese. Mix well.
Add-in the eggs gently, one at a time. Do not over mix the batter.
Let it bake for 25 to 30 minutes, or until cooked.

Nutrition: 88 kcal, Protein 2 g, Carbs 1 g, Fat 9 g

Sugar-Free Air Fried Chocolate Donut

Prep Time: 15 minutes   **Cook time: 15 minutes**
Servings: 32 donuts

Ingredients:

- 6 tbsp. Splenda
- 1 Cup flour
- Baking Soda: half tsp.

- 6 tbsp. Unsweetened Cocoa Powder
- 3 tbsp. of Butter
- 1 Egg

- Baking Powder: half tsp.
- 2 tbsp. of Unsweetened Chocolate chopped
- 1/4 cup white sugar-free Yogurt

Instructions

In a big mixing bowl, combine the baking powder, baking soda, and flour. Then add in the cocoa powder and sugar alternative.

In a mug, melt the butter and the cocoa.

Mix every 15 seconds and make sure they melt together and combine well. Set it aside to cool it down.

In that big mixing bowl from before, add in the yogurt and the egg. Add in the chocolate mixture. Cover the bowl with plastic wrap and let it chill in the refrigerator for 30 minutes.

To make the donut balls, take out the batter from the fridge. With the help of a tablespoon, scoop out sufficient batter so a donut ball will form with your hands. You can use oil on your hands if the dough is too sticky.

Spray the oil on the air fryer basket and sprinkle with flour and let it preheat to 350 F. Work in batches and add the balls in one single layer.

Let it bake for 10-12 minutes until they are done. To check doneness, try a toothpick if it comes out clean.
Take out from air fryer, let it cool and serve hot or cold.

Nutrition: 21 kcal, Protein 1 g, Carbs 1 g, Fat 2 g

Sugar-Free Low Carb Peanut Butter Cookies

Prep Time: 20 minutes   **Cook time:**
9 minutes
Servings: 24 cookies

Ingredients:

- *All-natural 100% peanut butter: 1 cup*
- *One whisked egg*
- *Liquid stevia drops: 1 teaspoon*
- *Sugar alternative: 1 cup*

Instructions
Mix all the ingredients into a dough. Make 24 balls with your hands from the combined dough.
On a cookie sheet or cutting board, press the dough balls with the help of a fork to form a crisscross pattern.
Add six cookies to the basket of air fryer in a single layer. Make sure the cookies are separated from each other. Cook in batches
Let them Air Fry, for 8-10 minutes, at 325. Take the basket out from the air fryer.
Let the cookies cool for one minute, then with care, take the cookies out.
Keep baking the rest of the cookies in batches.
Let them cool completely and serve.

Nutrition: 198 kcal, Protein 9.1 g, Carbs 5.9 g, Fat 16 g

Air Fryer Blueberry Muffins

Prep Time: 10 minutes

Cook time: 12 minutes

Servings: 8

Ingredients:

- *Half cup of sugar alternative*
- *One and 1/3 cup of flour*
- *1/3 cup of oil*

- *Two teaspoons of baking powder*
- *1/4 teaspoon of salt*
- *One egg*

- *Half cup of milk*
- *2/3 cup of frozen and thawed blueberries, or fresh*

Instructions

Let the air fryer preheat to 330 F.

In a large bowl, sift together baking powder, salt, sugar alternative, and flour. Mix well.

In another bowl, add milk, oil, and egg mix it well.

To the dry ingredients to the egg mix, mix until combined.

Add the blueberries carefully. Pour the mixture into muffin paper cups.

Cook muffins for 12-14 minutes, at 330 ° F.

Take out from the air fryer and let them cool before serving.

Nutrition: 211 kcal, Protein 9 g, Carbs 13 g, Fat 10 g

Air Fryer Sugar-Free Lemon Cookies

**Prep Time: 5
minutes
time: 5 minutes
Servings: 24 cookies**

Cook

Ingredients:

- *Half teaspoon of salt*
- *Half cup of coconut flour*
- *Half cup of unsalted butter softened*
- *Half teaspoon of liquid vanilla stevia*
- *Half cup of swerve granular sweetener*

- *One tablespoon lemon juice*
- *Two egg yolks*

For icing

- *Three tsp of lemon juice*
- *2/3 cup of Swerve confectioner's sweetener*

Instructions

In a stand mixer bowl, add coconut flour, salt and Swerve, mix until well combined.

Then add the butter (softened) to the dry ingredients, mix well. Add all the remaining ingredients but do not add in the yolks yet. Adjust the seasoning of lemon flavor and sweetness to your liking.

Add the yolks and combine well.

Lay a big piece of plastic wrap on a flat surface, put the batter in the center, roll around the dough and make it into a log form, for almost 12 inches. Keep this log in the fridge for 2-3 hours or overnight, if possible.

Let the oven preheat to 325 F. generously spray the air fryer basket, take the log out from plastic wrap.

Cut in 1/4 inch cookies, place them in the air fryer basket, but do not overcrowd the basket.

Bake for 3-five minutes, or until the cookies' edges become brown. Let it cool in the basket for two minutes, then take out. And let them cool on a wire rack.

Once all cookies are baked, pour the icing over.

Nutrition: 66 kcal, Protein 1 g, Carbs 2 g, Fat 6 g

Easy Air Fryer Brownies

Prep Time: 10 minutes   **Cook time: 10 minutes**
Servings: 2

Ingredients:

- *2 tbsp. of Baking Chips*
- *1/3 cup of Almond Flour*
- *One Egg*
- *Half teaspoon of Baking Powder*
- *3 tbsp. of Powdered Sweetener*
- *2 tbsp. of Cocoa Powder (Unsweetened)*

- *2 tbsp. of chopped Pecans*
- *4 tbsp. of melted Butter*

Instructions

Let the air fryer preheat to 350 F

In a large bowl, add cocoa powder, almond flour, powdered sweetener, and baking powder, give it a good mix.

Add melted butter and crack in the egg in the dry ingredients.

Mix well until combined and smooth. Fold in the chopped pecans and baking chips.

Take two ramekins to grease them well with softened butter. Add the batter.

Bake for ten minutes. Make sure to place them as far from the heat source from the top in the air fryer.

Take the brownies out from the air fryer and let them cool for five minutes.

Nutrition: 201 kcal, Protein 8 g, Carbs 13,1 g, Fat 10 g

Air Fryer Raspberry Cookies

Prep Time: 15 minutes   **Cook time: 10 minutes**
Servings: 10

Ingredients:

- *One teaspoon of baking powder*
- *One cup of almond flour*
- *Three tablespoons of natural low-calorie sweetener*
-
- *One large egg*
- *Three and a half tablespoons raspberry (reduced-sugar) preserves*

- *Four tablespoons of softened cream cheese*

Instructions
In a large bowl, add egg, baking powder, flour, sweetener, and cream cheese, mix well until a dough wet forms.

Chill the dough in the fridge for almost 20 minutes.

Let the air fryer preheat to 400 F, add the parchment paper to the air fryer basket.

Make ten balls from the dough and put them in the prepared air fryer basket.

With your clean hands, make an indentation from your thumb in the center of every cookie. Add one teaspoon of the raspberry preserve in the thumb hole.

Bake in the air fryer for seven minutes, or until light golden brown to your liking.

Let the cookies cool completely in the parchment paper for almost 15 minutes, or they will fall apart.

Nutrition: 111 kcal, Protein 3.6 g, Carbs 8.9 g, Fat 8.5 g

Air Fryer Apple Fritter

Prep Time: 10 minutes   **Cook time: 10 minutes**
Servings: 3

Ingredients:

- *Half apple peeled, finely chopped*
- *Half cup of All-Purpose Flour*
- *One teaspoon of Baking Powder*
- *1/4 teaspoon of Kosher Salt*
- *Half teaspoon of Ground Cinnamon*
- *2 Tbsp. of sugar alternative*
- *1/8 teaspoon of Ground Nutmeg*
- *3 Tbsp. of Greek Yogurt (Fat-Free)*
- *One tablespoon of Butter*

For the glaze

- *Two Tbsp. Of Powdered Sweetener*
- *Half tablespoon of Water*

Instructions

In a big mixing bowl, add baking powder, nutmeg, sugar alternative, flour, cinnamon, and salt. Mix it well.

With the help of a fork or cutter, slice the butter until crumbly.

Add the chopped apple and coat well, then add fat-free Greek yogurt.

Keep stirring until everything together, and a crumbly dough forms.

Put the dough on a clean surface and with your hands, knead it into a ball form.

Flatten the dough in an oval shape about a half-inch thick. It is okay, even if it's not the perfect size or shape.

Spray the basket of the air fryer with cooking spray generously. Put the dough in the air fry for 12-14 minutes at 375°F cook until light golden brown.

For making the glaze mix, the ingredients, and with the help of a brush, pour over the apple fritter when it comes out from the air fryer.

Slice and serve after cooling for 5 minutes.

Nutrition: 201 kcal, Protein 9.6 g, Carbs 13 g, Fat 11 g

Berry Cheesecake

Prep Time: 10 minutes   Cook time: 50 minutes
Servings: 8

Ingredients:

- *Half cup raspberries*
- *Two blocks of softened cream cheese, 8 ounce*
- *Vanilla extract: 1 teaspoon*
- *1/4 cup of strawberries*
- *Two eggs*
- *1/4 cup of blackberries*
- *One cup and 2 tbsp. of sweetener*

Instructions

In a big mixing bowl, whip the sweetener and cream cheese, mix with a whip until smooth and creamy. Then add vanilla extract and eggs, again mix well.

In a food processor or a blender, pulse the berries and fold into the cream cheese mix with two extra tbsp. of sweetener.

Take a springform pan and spray the oil generously, pour in the mixture. Put the pan in the air fryer, let it air fryer, and cook for 50 minutes at 300F.

Take out from the air fryer and cool a bit before chilling in the fridge. Keep in the fridge for 2-4 hours or as long as you have time.

Nutrition: 224 kcal, Protein 12 g, Carbs 17 g, Fat 16 g

Grain-free Molten Lava Cakes (Air Fryer)

Prep Time: 5 minutes   **Cook time: 10 minutes**
Servings: 2

Ingredients:

- *Two large eggs*
- *Half cup of dark chocolate chips*
- *2 tbsp. of coconut flour*
- *Two tablespoons of sugar substitute*
- *A dash of sea salt*
- *Half teaspoon of baking soda*
- *Butter and cocoa powder for two small ramekins*
- *1/4 cup of butter*

Instructions

Let the air fryer preheat to 370 degrees F.

Grease the ramekins with soft butter and sprinkle with cocoa powder. It will stick to the butter. Turn the ramekins upside down, so excess cocoa powder will fall out. Set it aside.

In a double boiler or microwave, safe bowl, melt the butter and chocolate chips together, stir every 15 seconds. Make sure to mix well to combine.

In a large bowl, crack the eggs and whisk with sugar substitute, mix well. Add in the baking soda, salt, and coconut flour. Gently fold everything. Then add the melted chocolate chip and butter mixture. Mix well, so everything combines.

Pour the batter in those two prepared ramekins.

Let them air fry for ten minutes. Then take them out from the air fryer and let it cool for 3-4 minutes.

Nutrition: 216 kcal, Protein 9.9 g, Carbs 13 g, Fat 12 g

Tahini Oatmeal Chocolate Chunk Cookies

Prep Time: 10 minutes   **Cook time: 5 minutes**
Servings: 8

Ingredients:

- *1/3 cup of tahini*
- *1/4 cup of walnuts*
- *1/4 cup of maple syrup*
- *1/4 cup of Chocolate chunks*
- *1/4 tsp of sea salt*
- *Two tablespoons of almond flour*

- *One teaspoon of vanilla*
- *1 cup of gluten-free oat flakes*
- *One teaspoon of cinnamon*

Instructions
Let the air fryer Preheat to 350 F.

In a big bowl, add the maple syrup, cinnamon, the tahini, salt, and vanilla. Mix well. Then add in the walnuts, oat flakes, and almond meal. Then fold the chocolate chips gently.

Take a full tablespoon of mixture, separate into eight amounts.

Line the air fryer basket with parchment paper and place cookies in one single layer.

Let them cook for 5-6 minutes at 350 F, air fry for more minutes if you like them crispy.

Nutrition: 185.4 kcal, Protein 12 g, Carbs 18.4 g, Fat 11 g

Eggless & Vegan Cake

Prep Time: 5 minutes   **Cook time: 15 minutes**
Servings: 8

Ingredients:

- *Olive Oil: 2 Tbsp.*
- *All-Purpose Flour: 1/4 Cup*
- *Cocoa Powder: 2 Tbsp.*
- *Baking Soda: 1/8 Tsp*
- *Sugar substitute: 3 Tbsp.*
- *One tablespoon of Warm Water*
- *Milk: 3 Tbsp.*
- *Two Drops of Vanilla Extract*
- *4 Raw Almonds for decoration – roughly chopped*
- *A Pinch of Salt*

Instructions

Let the air fryer preheat to 370°F for at least two minutes.

In a large bowl, add sugar substitute, milk, water, and oil. Whisk until a smooth batter forms.

Now add salt, all-purpose flour, cocoa powder, and baking soda, sift them into wet ingredients, and mix to form a paste.

Spray a four-inch baking pan with oil and pour the batter into it. Then add in the chopped up almonds on top of it.

Put the baking pan in the preheated air fryer. And cook for ten minutes.

Check the doneness with a toothpick. If it comes out clean, they are done.

Take out from the air fryer and let it cool completely before slicing.

Nutrition: 121 kcal, Protein 2 g, Carbs 17.9 g, Fat 8 g

Banana Muffins in Air Fryer

Prep Time: 10 minutes   **Cook time: 10 minutes**
Servings: 8

Ingredients:

Wet Mix

- *3 tbsp. of milk*
- *Four Cavendish size, ripe bananas*
- *Half cup sugar alternative*
- *One teaspoon of vanilla essence*
- *Two large eggs*

Dry Mix

- *One teaspoon of baking powder*
- *One and a 1/4 cup of whole wheat flour*
- *One teaspoon of baking soda*
- *One teaspoon of cinnamon*
- *2 tbsp. of cocoa powder*
- *One teaspoon of salt*

Optional

- *Chopped walnuts: 1 handful*
- *Fruits, Dried slices*

Instructions

With the fork, in a bowl, mash up the bananas, add all the wet ingredients to it, and mix well.

Sift all the dry ingredients so they combine well. Add into the wet ingredients. Carefully fold both ingredients together.

Then add in the chopped walnuts, and slices of dried up fruits.

Let the air fryer preheat to 260°F.

Spray muffin cups with oil generously, and add the batter into.

Air fryer them for at least half an hour, or until a toothpick comes out clean.

Take out from the air fryer and let them cool down before serving.

Nutrition: 211 kcal, Protein 12 g, Carbs 18 g, Fat 12 g

30-DAY MEAL PLAN

This meal plan is designed to help you achieve the best health possible. Hope you enjoy these delicious recipes that will keep your belly full and glucose level under control for days to come.

Taking inspiration from the recipes described in this cookbook, the meal plan is valid for 1000 days.

Week 1

Monday (Day 1)
Breakfast: Bell Peppers Frittata
Lunch: Lemon Rosemary Chicken
Snack: Air-Fryer Kale Chips with dipping
Dinner: Air Fryer Pork Taquitos

Tuesday (Day 2)
Breakfast: Air Fryer Crisp Egg Cups
Lunch: Air-Fried Rosemary Garlic Grilled Prawns
Snack: Air Fryer Buffalo Cauliflower with dipping
Dinner: Air Fried Empanadas

Wednesday (Day 3)
Breakfast: Asparagus Frittata
Lunch: Crispy Air Fryer Fish
Snack: Air Fryer Onion Rings with dipping
Dinner: Air Fryer Lemon Garlic Shrimp

Thursday (Day 4)
Breakfast: Mushroom Oatmeal
Lunch: Chicken Fajitas
Snack: Air Fryer Chicken Nuggets
Dinner: Sriracha & Honey Tossed Calamari

Friday (Day 5)
Breakfast: Air Fryer Egg Rolls
Lunch: Air Fryer Delicata Squash
Snack: Zucchini Parmesan Chips
Dinner: Air Fryer Crispy Fish Sandwich

Saturday (Day 6)
Breakfast: Air Fryer Salmon cakes
Lunch: Air Fryer Popcorn Chicken
Snack: Zucchini Gratin
Dinner: Air Fryer Lemon Pepper Shrimp

Sunday (Day 7)
Breakfast: Air Fryer Egg Rolls
Lunch: Air Fryer Crispy Fish Sticks
Snack: One Blueberry Muffin
Dinner: Air-Fried Buttermilk Chicken

Week 2

Monday (Day 8)
Breakfast: Air-Fried Spinach Frittata
Lunch: Crispy Air Fryer Brussels Sprouts
Snack: Slice of Vegan Cake
Dinner: Air Fryer Turkey Breast

Tuesday (Day 9)
Breakfast: Mushroom Omelet
Lunch: Coconut Shrimp
Dinner: Juicy Turkey Burgers with Zucchini

Wednesday (Day 10)
Breakfast: Mushroom Oatmeal
Lunch: Air Fryer Fish and Chips
Snack: Slice of Berry Cheesecake
Dinner: Air Fryer Meatloaf

Thursday (Day 11)
Breakfast: Lemon-Garlic Tofu
Lunch: Air Fryer Hamburger
Snack: Slice of Carrot Cake
Dinner: Air-Fried Buttermilk Chicken

Friday (Day 12)
Breakfast: Air-fryer omelet
Lunch: Air Fried Empanadas
Snack: Zucchini Chips
Dinner: Air Fry Rib-Eye Steak

Saturday (Day 13)
Breakfast: Breakfast Bombs
Lunch: Orange Chicken Wings
Snack: Low Carb Pork Dumplings with Dipping Sauce
Dinner: Air Fryer Chicken & Broccoli

Sunday (Day 14)
Breakfast: Air-fryer baked eggs

Lunch: Air Fryer Low Carb Chicken Bites
Snack: Half Sugar Free Brownie
Dinner: Air-Fried Turkey Breast with Maple Mustard Glaze

Week 3

Monday (Day 15)
Breakfast: Crisp egg cups
Lunch: Sweet potato fries
Snack: One Apple Cider Donut
Dinner: Air Fryer Whole Wheat Crusted Pork Chops

Tuesday (Day 16)
Breakfast: Vegan Breakfast Sandwich
Lunch: Air Fryer Delicata Squash
Snack: Air Fryer Kale Chips
Dinner: Air-Fried Chicken Pie

Wednesday (Day 17)
Breakfast: Vegan mashed potato bowl
Lunch: Chicken Fajitas
Snack: One blueberry muffin
Dinner: Garlic Parmesan Crusted Salmon

Thursday (Day 18)
Breakfast: Toad in the hole tarts
Lunch: Air Fryer Low Carb Chicken Bites
Snack: Avocado fries
Dinner: Air Fryer Hamburger

Friday (Day 19)
Breakfast: Breakfast bombs

Lunch: Air Fryer Chicken & Broccoli
Snack: Onion rings
Dinner: Air Fryer Sesame Seeds Fish Fillet

Saturday (Day 20)
Breakfast: Mushroom Omelet
Lunch: Garlic Parmesan Crusted Salmon
Snack: Roasted corn
Dinner: Chicken Fajitas

Sunday (Day 21)
Breakfast: Avocado Egg Rolls
Lunch: Air Fryer Lemon Pepper Shrimp
Snack: Zucchini Parmesan Chips
Dinner: Air Fry Rib-Eye Steak

Week 4

Monday (Day 22)
Breakfast: Apple fritter
Lunch: Air-Fried Rosemary Garlic Grilled Prawns
Dinner: Mustard Glazed Air Fryer Pork Tenderloin

Tuesday (Day 23)
Breakfast: Lemon-Garlic Tofu
Lunch: Air Fryer Turkey Breast Tenderloin
Snack: Small slice of sugar-free berry cheesecake
Dinner: Air Fryer Lemon Pepper Shrimp

Wednesday (Day 24)
Breakfast: Vegan Breakfast Sandwich

Lunch: Air Fryer Chicken & Broccoli
Snack: Slice of Carrot Cake
Dinner: Air-Fried Rosemary Garlic Grilled Prawns

Thursday (Day 25)
Breakfast: Egg Air-Fryer Omelet
Lunch: Air Fryer Southwest Chicken
Snack: Air-fry Brownie
Dinner: Air Fryer Sesame Seeds Fish Fillet

Friday (Day 26)
Breakfast: Slice of eggless and vegan cake
Lunch: Air Fryer Low Carb Chicken Bites
Snack: Kale chips
Dinner: Air Fryer Turkey Breast Tenderloin

Saturday (Day 27)
Breakfast: Bell Pepper Frittata
Lunch: Air-Fried Buttermilk Chicken
Snack: Chicken Nuggets
Dinner: Air Fry Rib-Eye Steak

Sunday (Day 28)
Breakfast: Air-fryer Spanakopita Bites
Lunch: Orange Chicken Wings
Snack: One peanut butter cookie
Dinner: Air Fryer Hamburger

Week 5

Monday (Day 29)

Breakfast: Toad in the hole Tart
Lunch: Crab cakes
Snack: Air Fryer Roasted Corn
Dinner: Air Fried Empanadas

Tuesday (Day 30)
Breakfast: Banana muffin with coffee
Lunch: Lemon Rosemary Chicken
Snack: Egg rolls
Dinner: Air Fryer Delicata Squash

Printed by Amazon Italia Logistica S.r.l.
Torrazza Piemonte (TO), Italy

61741394R00150